How to Integrate the Curricula

SECOND EDITION

by

Robin Fogarty

SkyLight
Professional
Development

How to Integrate the Curricula, Second Edition

Published by SkyLight Professional Development
2626 S. Clearbrook Dr., Arlington Heights, Illinois 60005-5310
800-348-4474 or 847-290-6600
Fax 847-290-6609
info@skylightedu.com
http://www.skylightedu.com

President: Carol Luitjens
Executive Editor: Chris Jaeggi
Acquisitions Editor: Jean Ward
Editor: Anne Kaske
Project Editor: Dara Lee Howard
Assistant Editor: Carrie Straka
Book Designer: Bruce Leckie
Illustrator: David Stockman
Editorial Coordinator: Donna Ramirez
Production Supervisor: Bob Crump

LCCCN 2001099349
1-57517-540-1

3013V
Item Number 2399

ZYXWVUTSRQPONMLKJIHGFEDCBA
10 09 08 07 06 05 04 03 02   15 14 13 12 11 10 9 8 7 6 5 4 3 2 1

There are
one-story intellects,
two-story intellects, and
three-story intellects with skylights.

All fact collectors, who have no aim beyond their facts, are
one-story minds.

Two-story minds
compare, reason, generalize,
using the labors of the fact collectors
as well as their own.

Three-story minds
idealize, imagine, predict—their best illumination
comes from above,

through the **skylight**.

—Oliver Wendell Holmes

SkyLight
Professional
Development

Dedication

To three integrated learners I know:

The poet, who navigates the stars;
The writer, who touches the soul; and
The inventor, who notes nature's ways.

SkyLight Professional Development

Contents

HOW TO
INTEGRATE
THE CURRICULA

SkyLight Professional Development

Foreword

In the spirit of continuous learning, Dr. Robin Fogarty has added new insight into this second edition of *How to Integrate the Curricula*. Her initial contributions to the field of education were to give teachers clear and practical images and exercises provoking new perspectives on curriculum making. Fogarty builds and adds useful suggestions that deepen the work. She has added refined practices, engaging strategies, and targeted research references to support her models for curriculum design.

Ultimately, this is a practical book supported by strong theoretical underpinnings. A useful tool for inservice workshops and personal intructional growth, teachers and staff developers will find the book extremely helpful. Dr. Fogarty has a knack for cutting directly to key points in an engaging style. Certainly the goal of any professional improvement plan is to eventually help our learners—*How to Integrate the Curricula* can aid educators to assist all learners in the classroom to be thoughtful, creative, and mindful.

Dr. Heidi Hayes Jacobs
President, Curriculum Designers
Rye, New York
January, 2002

Acknowledgments

I remember reading once in someone's introduction that "This book took a year—plus a lifetime—to write!" The thoughts shared here represent an accumulation of ideas over time and present the core of the integrated learner model. Learners must constantly and continually make connections. As they proceed on their journeys, they single-mindedly dig into an idea and at the same time they network with others for breadth across related fields. As a result, concepts come into focus and emerge as beliefs that propel learners even further along on their chosen path and into never-ending circles of expert associates. In my work with curriculum and cognitive instruction, there are two camps of expert associates that have influenced my thinking about how to integrate the curricula: the expert *theorists* and the expert *practitioners*.

In the theorists' camp, I'd like to acknowledge Heidi Hayes Jacobs for providing the initial impetus for this work. Her chapter, "Design Options for an Integrated Curriculum" (in Jacobs 1989), acted as a catalyst for the ideas presented in this book.

In addition, I'm especially grateful to David Perkins for an illuminating discussion on finding fertile themes with which to integrate curricula. With his rich criteria, this thematic model takes on new integrity. In the absence of applied criteria, topical themes are often superficial, with content artificially included or excluded accordingly. David's "lenses" provide the needed rigor. In addition, thanks go to David for the idea of the characters placed in a school setting. This sparked the inclusion of the cartoons that appear throughout the book.

Finally, also in the theorists' camp, I'd like to thank Art Costa for his initial review of the integrated models and his timely suggestion for one that illustrates how a teacher targets several ideas in a single lesson or nests several ideas together—thus, the nested model that appears as integrated model 3.

Now, in the practitioners' camp, there are four distinct expert flanks: teachers from Carpentersville, Illinois; teachers from the Waterford School District, Michigan; teachers from the Richmond School District, British Columbia, Canada; and teachers from Virginia Beach Schools, Virginia.

Elementary and middle school teachers from Carpentersville, Illinois, worked on models to help integrate the curricula for lessons and learners. Some of their lesson designs appear as examples in this book. My thanks for their early efforts with me in exploring this idea of an integrated curriculum: Carol Bonebrake, Jane Atherton, Suzanne Raymond, Barbara Bengston, Al Eck, Kathleen Vehring, Roseanne Day, Nancy Blackman, Clifford Berutti, Linda Morning, Diane Gray, and Terri Pellant.

My thanks to Julie Casteel and her teachers in Michigan, especially Al Monetta, Chris Brakke, Lori Broughton, and Sue Barber, who provided the topics to fill in the first model in Figure 1.1 of this book. At SkyLight Professional Development, we know that "If Julie is doing it, it must be the next educational innovation." A pioneer practitioner leading the thinking skills movement into action research teams, she is once again on the cutting edge with the integrated learning idea. My thanks to both Julie and her risk-taking staff for letting me test the models with real teachers.

My sincere thanks to my friends and colleagues in Canada. First to Carol-Lyn Sakata who brought me there, then to Bruce Beairsto, David Shore, and Darlene Macklam, for introducing me to the teachers of Richmond. Their heroic efforts to implement a visionary provincial document, "Year 2000: A Framework for Learning," inspired my work. I am especially indebted to one teacher, Heather MacLaren. She asked her seventh graders to prepare to talk at their parent conferences about what they had done that year and how all the things they had learned overlapped and were connected. The students' intricate Venn diagrams provided graphic representations of integrating the curricula as perceived through the eyes of the learners. These drawings sparked my own thinking about creative, integrative models.

In addition, working with eighty teachers in a summer workshop in Richmond called Teaching for Transfer, John Barell, David Perkins, and I (with the help of Captain Meta Cognition, our superhero) had a first stab at trying to help teachers sift out curricular priorities. This, too, served as an initial springboard for my ideas about how to integrate the curricula. Also,

special thanks to Monica Pamer, Gina Rae, and Jacquie Anderson for their conversations and encouragement.

The fourth set of practitioners represent the Virginia Beach Schools. Their work with Student Learning Standards in designing performance tasks illuminates the process of designing integrated curricula with the "standards in mind." For their robust performance tasks, I am grateful.

Finally, I would be remiss if I neglected to mention my internal network of colleagues. I thank Jim Bellanca for his faith in me and my ideas; Bruce Leckie for the *design* part that not only shaped but propelled the *writing* part; David Stockman for his cover art and cartoons; Julie Noblitt, Dara Lee Howard, and Anne Kaske for their editors' eyes; Donna Ramirez for her ability to decipher my revisions; and Jean Ward for encouraging me to revise the first edition.

Introduction

To the young mind every thing is individual, stands by itself. By and by, it finds how to join two things and see in them one nature; then three, then three thousand; and so, tyrannized over by its own unifying instinct, it goes on tying things together, diminishing anomalies, discovering roots running underground whereby contrary and remote things cohere and flower out from one stem. . . . The astronomer discovers that geometry, a pure abstraction of the human mind, is the measure of planetary motion. The chemist finds proportions and intelligible method throughout matter; and science is nothing but the finding of analogy, identity, in the most remote parts.—EMERSON

What Is This Book All About?

To help the "young mind . . . [discover] roots running underground whereby contrary and remote things cohere and flower out from one stem" is at once the mission of the teacher and of the learner. To that end, this book presents models to connect and integrate the curricula.

What does integrating the curricula mean? Does it mean sifting out the parcels of each overloaded discipline and focusing on the priorities in depth? (Cellular Model)

Does it mean integrating or connecting yesterday's lesson to today's topic? Or relating all issues studied in the biology class to the concept of evolution? Or does it mean utilizing concepts such as *power* and *isolation* throughout the social studies topics? (Connected Model)

Does integrated curricula mean targeting multidimensional skills and concepts into one lesson (Nested Model), or rearranging the sequence of when a topic is taught to coincide with a parallel topic in another content? (Sequenced Model) Does it mean integrating one subject with another through the learner's conceptual eye (Shared Model), or selecting an overall

theme (such as *persistence* or *argument*), or a simple topic (such as *transportation*) to use as a thematic umbrella? Or is it selecting a book, an era, or an artist and weaving those themes into the fabric of the discipline? (Webbed Model)

Does integrated curricula mean integrating the content of what is taught with cognitive tools and cooperative strategies that cross disciplines and spill into life situations? (Threaded Model) Or does it encompass interdisciplinary team planning in which conceptual overlaps become the common focus across departments? (Integrated Model)

Does integrating the curricula mean exploiting integrative threads within the learner to connect past experiences and prior knowledge with new information and experiences (Immersed Model), or does it mean reaching out to build bonds with other experts through networking? (Networked Model)

The answer, of course, is that integrating the curricula can be any or all—and more—of the aforementioned models. Each teacher and each learner views the integration process differently.

Why Bother?

Four winds of change drive the need to create integrated curriculum. These winds come from four distinct directions. The north and south are the ideas of the educational *theorists* and the challenges of the *practitioners;* the east and west represent the concerns of *parents* and the perspective of the *students* themselves. From the theorists come data on teaching, learning, and the human brain; from the practitioners, frustration with an over-crowded standards-based and test-driven curriculum. From opposite vectors, parents are concerned about student preparation and readiness for real-world issues, while the children themselves see learning as fractured and not very relevant. A closer look at these crosswinds of change reveals their impact on the current education climate of school reform in our nation's schools.

The Theorists: Research on the Brain and Learning

Supporting the concept of a more connected, integrated curricula is a research base that delineates twelve principles of the brain and learning (Caine and Caine 1994). Note in Figure 0.1 that some of these principles are common sense, others reinforce accepted pedagogy, and still others are just gaining acceptance in the world of cognition.

Caines' Twelve Principles of the Brain and Learning

1. Learning is enhanced by challenge.
2. Emotions are critical to patterning.
3. Learning involves both focused and peripheral perception.
4. The brain processes parts and whole simultaneously.
5. The brain has a spatial memory system and a set of systems for rote learning.
6. The brain is a parallel processor.
7. Learning engages the entire physiology.
8. Each brain is unique.
9. Understanding and remembering occur best when the facts are embedded in natural, spatial memory.
10. The search for meaning is innate.
11. The search for meaning occurs through patterning.
12. Learning always involves conscious and unconscious processes.

(Adapted from Caine and Caine 1994, *Making Connections: Teaching and the Human Brain.*)

Figure 0.1

Creating the Learning Environment

The first three principles create the learning environment.

1. *Learning is enhanced by challenge.* The brain learns optimally when appropriately challenged and reacts viscerally when it senses threat. Therefore, a safe, rich environment fosters a state of "relaxed alertness" for learning, whereas threatening experiences, such as testing situations, often create a state of fear and anxiety.

2. *Emotions are critical to patterning.* Emotions and cognition cannot be separated. When emotions kick in, the brain pays attention, and that attention is necessary for memory and learning. Therefore, a positive emotional hook, such as an intriguing question, enhances learning.

3. *Learning involves both focused and peripheral perception.* The brain responds to the entire sensory context. Therefore, in an enriched environment, peripheral information can be purposely organized to facilitate learning. The use of learning centers, study stations, or even the way teachers represent information on the board are organizational tools that enhance memory and learning.

Using Explicit and Implicit Memory Systems

Principles 4 and 5 involve the memory systems.

4. *The brain processes parts and whole simultaneously.* Bilateralization of right and left hemisphere processing, although inextricably linked for interaction, allows the brain to reduce information into parts and, at the same time, to perceive and work with the information as a whole. Therefore, immediate application of direct instruction of skills and concepts allows the learner to perceive the information from both perspectives.

5. *The brain has a spatial memory system and a set of systems for rote learning.* There is natural, spatial memory that needs no rehearsal and affords instant memory, and there are facts and skills that are dealt with in isolation and do require rehearsal. Therefore, teaching must focus on the personal world of the learner to make learning relevant, as well as rote memorization techniques to foster long-term learning for transfer. Rote memorization requires more conscious effort to remember because the facts may have little meaning or relevance to the learner. When the brain senses that there is no need to remember, it tends to let go of the information. Therefore, rote memorization of isolated facts often needs more explicit work to learn and recall information, whereas spatial memory has built-in cues that help in the retrieval of information.

Processing Incoming Information

Processing is supported by four principles.

6. *The brain is a parallel processor.* Thoughts, emotions, imagination, and pre-dispositions operate simultaneously. Therefore, optimal learning results from orchestrating the learning experience to address multiple operations in the brain.

7. *Learning engages the entire physiology.* Learning is as natural as breathing, yet neuron growth, nourishment, and emotional interactions are integrally related to the perception and interpretation of experiences. Therefore, stress management, nutrition, exercise, and relaxation become the focus of the teaching and learning process.

8. *Each brain is unique.* Although most brains have a similar set of systems for sensing, feeling, and thinking, the set is integrated differently in each brain. Therefore, teaching that is multifaceted with inherent choices and options for the learner fosters optimal learning.

SkyLight Professional Development

9. *Understanding and remembering occur best when the facts are embedded in natural, spatial memory.* Specific items are given meaning when embedded in ordinary experiences, such as learning grammar and punctuation and applying the learning to writing; therefore, experiential learning that affords opportunities for embedded learning is necessary for optimal learning.

Making Meaning

The final three principles address the brain's way of making meaning.

10. *The search for meaning is innate.* The search for meaning cannot be stopped, only channeled and focused. Therefore, classrooms need stability and routine as well as novelty and challenge, and the learning can be shepherded explicitly through mediation and reflection.

11. *The search for meaning occurs through patterning.* The brain has a natural capacity to integrate vast amounts of seemingly unrelated information. Therefore, when teaching invokes integrated, thematically reflective approaches, learning is more brain compatible and is, subsequently, enhanced.

12. *Learning always involves conscious and unconscious processes.* Enormous amounts of unconscious processing go on beneath the surface of awareness. Some of this happens when a person is awake, and much of it continues when a person is at rest or even asleep. Therefore, teaching needs to be organized experientially and reflectively to benefit maximally from the deep processing.

In addition, each brain has a unique profile of intelligences: verbal/ linguistic, visual/spatial, interpersonal/social, intrapersonal/introspective, musical/rhythmic, logical/mathematical, bodily/kinesthetic, and naturalist (Gardner 1983).

What does this forceful wind of change bring to the educational agenda? It brings the idea of orchestrating the curriculum into complex experiences in which students are immersed in multiple ways of learning and knowing (Kovalic 1993). These robust curriculum models include integrated, thematic instruction and ongoing projects and performances, such as a student-produced newspaper, a school musical, or a service learning project to eliminate the graffiti in the community (Caine and Caine 1991, 1994). This seamless learning—curricula that find the "roots running underground"—fosters connection-making for lessons and learners.

The Practitioners: Abandonment of an Overloaded Curriculum and Adherence to Standards of Learning

One university professor tells his pre-med students, "By the time you graduate and become practicing physicians, 50 percent of what we've taught you will be obsolete . . . and we don't know which half that will be" (Fogarty and Bellanca 1989).

Curriculum overload is a reality that teachers from kindergarten to college face every day. Drug and alcohol education, AIDS awareness, consumer issues, marriage and family living, computer technology, Web and Internet training, character education, and violence prevention programs have all been added over the years to an already content-packed curriculum. There is no end to it. The myriad content standards of the various disciplines and the process standards or life skills—thinking, organizing, assessing information, problem solving and decision making, cooperation, collaboration, and teamwork—inundate the expanding curriculum.

Meeting Standards with Integrated Curricula

There is some confusion about how to meet the spectrum of content standards required by the various states. Some think that each standard must be addressed discretely and within a particular discipline. Yet, common sense tells us that if educators try to approach the standards by laying them end to end in a sequential discipline-based map, we would need to add at least two more years to the schooling cycle. The only way the compendium of standards can possibly be met is by clustering the standards into logical bundles and addressing them in an explicit but integrated fashion.

It's not standards *or* curriculum, but rather, standards *and* curriculum. Standards help to prioritize content teaching in an overloaded, fragmented, and sometimes outdated curriculum. Standards provide the foundation for what students need to know and be able to do. Well-designed standards help set the curricular priorities necessary for an integrated, coherent, and authentic curriculum.

With this solid foundation firmly in place, decisions about curriculum become seamless as teachers decide what to selectively abandon and/or judiciously include in their planning. Standards champion the cause of a more connected, more relevant, more purposeful curriculum at all levels of schooling.

SkyLight Professional Development

Sample standards of learning appear in Figure 0.2 to illustrate the types of learning goals contained in typical state standards for student achievement. A cursory look at these representative standards illustrates the broad strokes of the standards and the ease of integration of standards as they are clustered and layered within robust learning.

Sample Standards of Learning

Sample Communications Arts Standards
Students will acquire a solid foundation that includes knowledge of and proficiency in:
1. speaking and writing standard English (grammar, punctuation, and spelling)
2. reading and evaluating fiction (poetry and drama) and nonfiction (biographies, newspapers, technical manuals)
3. relationships between language and culture

Sample Mathematics Standards
Students will acquire a solid foundation that includes knowledge of and proficiency in:
1. addition, subtraction, multiplication, and division and other number sense
2. data analysis, probability, and statistics
3. mathematical systems, geometry, and number theory

Sample Science Standards
Students will acquire a solid foundation that includes knowledge of and proficiency in:
1. properties and principles of matter and energy, force and motion
2. characteristics and interactions of living organisms
3. processes of scientific inquiry

Sample Social Studies Standards
Students will acquire a solid foundation that includes knowledge of and proficiency in:
1. economic principles
2. principles of democracy and processes of governance
3. geographical study and analysis

Figure 0.2 (continued on next page)

Sample Fine Arts Standards

Students will acquire a solid foundation that includes knowledge of and proficiency in:
1. processes and techniques of production, exhibition, and performances
2. principles and elements of different art forms
3. interrelationships of visual and performing arts

Sample Health/Physical Education Standards

Students will acquire a solid foundation that includes knowledge of and proficiency in:
1. structures of, functions of, and relationships among human body systems
2. principles and practices of mental health
3. principles of movement and fitness

(Adapted from Missouri Department of Elementary and Secondary Education 1996)

Figure 0.2

This book promotes the concept of a standards-based and an integrated curriculum that is reflective of lifelong learning. With standards as the guide for rigorous and relevant curricular decisions, readers may use the inventories in the introduction (Figures 0.7 and 0.8) to determine what they are already doing to foster an integration of concepts, skills, and attitudes across the disciplines.

These quick inventories introduce readers to the ten models that shape integration of the curricula in myriad ways. As readers learn about the models described in this book, they discover ways to prioritize curriculum concerns, methods for sequencing and mapping curricular content, templates for webbing themes across disciplines, techniques for threading life skills into all content areas, and strategies to immerse students in content through self-selected, personally relevant learning experiences.

The focus on standards-based curriculum begins the conversation about what students need to know and be able to do. The concept of integrated curriculum continues the conversation with practical ways to transform that learning into real-life experiences that transfer effortlessly into future applications. Remember, it's not standards *or* integrated curriculum, but *both* standards *and* integrated curriculum that lead to students who are well-prepared for a world we as their teachers may never know.

With a multitude of standards as the goal, coverage of content, of course, is an ongoing concern as traditional evaluations, such as "the test," are supplemented with more authentic assessments, such as portfolios and performances. Yet, as Hunter (1971) so aptly put it in a story she tells, "Covering the curriculum is like taking a passenger to the airport—you rush around and get to the airport on time, but you leave the passenger at home." In other words, a teacher finishes the book or curriculum but wonders if the students came too. In the flurry of covering the content standards, to prepare students for "the test," some students are left far behind. As one student said, "Mrs. Smith, may I be excused, my brain is full?"

What does this powerful wind of change mean for the schools? It means educators need to seek ways to "selectively abandon and judiciously include" standards in the curriculum (Costa in Fogarty 1991). The standards are the goals of the curriculum approach, *within* a single discipline, *across* content areas, and *in* the mind of the learner.

The Parents: What Will Our Children Need Twenty-Five Years from Now?

A father of a thirteen year old describes the typical, cellular model of schooling in which a grade eight student brings home "thirty examples to do for math homework, twenty minutes of trombone practice, an autobiography to complete, irregular French verbs to learn for a test, and a chapter to read in the science text" (Anonymous in Fogarty 1991). He goes on, "There is a need to examine what students learn under these circumstances. Students may opt to do all of it, do some of it or do none of it. Surely we must wonder: what do we want kids to know twenty-five years from now? And, we must create the organizational structure that eliminates obstacles and enables students to grow and learn."

This wind of change means that students need schooling for a lifetime, not just for the test (Bellanca and Fogarty 1991). In terms of relevant learning for life, one parent relates a comment from her son, who told her, "I have a million things on my mind and not one of them turned up on the test."

Yes, educators want all students to meet the learning standards, and they want them to pass the test, but, in the end, they really want students to be able to function effectively in life. Interestingly, one critical element of integrated learning is in the lifelike projects that are relevant and meaningful to students.

The Students: Education Is a Vaccination

A student once told me, "Education is like a vaccination. Math is not English. English is not science. Science is not history. A subject is something you take once and need never take again. I had my shot of biology" (Fogarty 1993). While subject matter content falls neatly into those discipline-based departments, students, unfortunately, do not compartmentalize themselves or their learning that readily.

Learning is incidental, inductive (Kovalic 1993); it's holistic and it's interactive (Bellanca and Fogarty 1991). Students learn the complex skill of language from their interactions with the language in genuine and authentic episodes. Baby talk disappears because other people do not talk that way. The comment, "We learned about unregular verbs today," will be self-corrected to conform with standard English because students desperately want to say things "the right way." And, they learn much of this naturally in integrated, cross-ability groupings of siblings and peers.

What does this wind of change mean? It means a shift toward more holistic, experiential learning for children. It means problem-based learning, case studies, performance tasks, service learning, apprenticeships, and internships. Learning is a function of experience. Therefore, teachers must create the experiences for the learners.

How Can the Curriculum Be Integrated?

Each teacher and each learner views the integration process differently. Yet, there is a common vision encompassing three distinct dimensions that is accepted by a large number of educators as depicted in Figure 0.3.

The *vertical spiral* represents the spiraling curricula built into most texts and standards documents as content is integrated and revisited through the K–12 grades. Mastery of certain materials is expected at each level in preparation for building on that material for the next concepts at subsequent levels. Integration occurs vertically throughout the schooling years.

The *horizontal band* represents the breadth and depth of learning in a given subject. As different subjects are approached, explored, and learned within each discipline, a cumulative effect is anticipated. Students are to expand their conceptual bases for future learning in related fields: one math concept builds toward the next as ideas are integrated within a discipline.

How to Integrate the Curricula: Three Dimensions

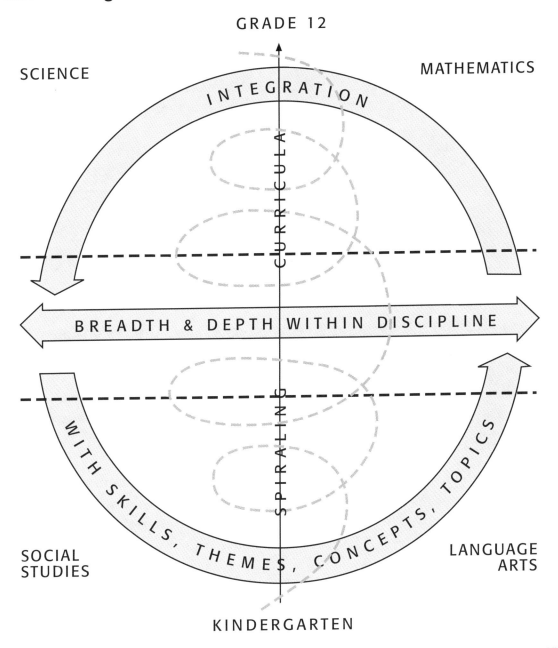

Figure 0.3

Finally, the *circle* represents the integration of skills, themes, concepts, and topics across disciplines as similarities are noted. These explicit connections are used to enhance the learning in a holistic manner as students link ideas from one subject to ideas in another subject.

How to Integrate the Curricula

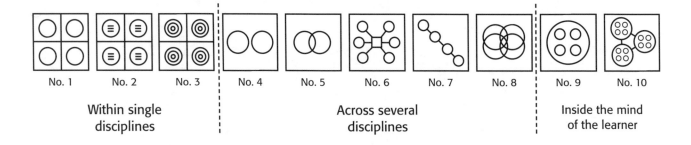

Figure 0.4

In summary, both integration *within* a discipline and integration *across* disciplines are necessary to fully integrate the curricula.

To further explore this idea, this book presents detailed discussions on a range of models (see Figure 0.4 for a graphical overview). Beginning with an exploration within single disciplines, at the left end of the spectrum, and continuing with models that integrate across several disciplines, the continuum ends with models that integrate within the learner and finally across networks of other learners.

These ten models provide a tool for teachers and teacher leaders to inventory what they are already doing in their classrooms and schools to integrate the curricula. Figure 0.5 identifies the ten views for integrating the curricula. See Figures 0.6 and 0.7 for the interactive charts of the ten models.

In Conclusion

The winds of change are stronger than we think. The brain research, the off-loading of an overloaded curriculum, the emergence of a standards-based curriculum, the need for the life skills of thinking and collaborating, and the call for learner-centered schools are moving forces in the educational world today. These winds signal the need for integrated, rich, and robust curricula that serve as *gateways* to lifelong learning—not as *gatekeepers* that block the pathways for particular learners. These are the forces that are moving educators toward integrated, holistic, and authentic kinds of learning. The winds will not calm. Change is in the air. It is imminent.

Toward an Integrated Curriculum

Ten Views for Integrating the Curricula: How Do You See It?

1 **Cellular**
Periscope—one direction; one sighting; narrow focus on single discipline or content area

Description
The traditional model of separate and distinct disciplines, as depicted by student learning standards in each discipline area.

Example
The teacher applies this view in mathematics, science, social studies, language arts or sciences, humanities, fine and practical arts.

2 **Connected**
Opera glass—details of one discipline; focus on subtleties and interconnections

Description
Within each subject area, course content is connected topic to topic, concept to concept, one year's work to the next, and relates ideas explicitly.

Example
The teacher relates the concept of fractions to decimals, which in turn relates to money, grades, etc.

3 **Nested**
3-D glasses—multiple dimensions to one scene, topic or unit

Description
Within each subject area, the teacher targets multiple skills: a social skill, a thinking skill, and a content-specific skill based on standards.

Example
The teacher designs the unit on photosynthesis to simultaneously target consensus seeking (social skill), sequencing (thinking skill), and plant life cycle (science content).

4 **Sequenced**
Eye glasses—varied internal content framed by broad, related topics

Description
Topics or units of study are rearranged and sequenced to coincide with one another. Similar ideas are taught in concert while remaining separate subjects.

Example
An English teacher presents a historical novel depicting a particular period while the history teacher teaches that same historical period.

5 **Shared**
Binoculars—two disciplines that share overlapping concepts and skills

Description
Shared planning takes place in two disciplines in which overlapping concepts or ideas emerge as organizing elements.

Example
Science and mathematics teachers use data collection, charting, and graphing as shared concepts.

6 **Webbed**
Telescope—broad view of an entire constellation as one theme, webbed to the various elements

Description
Webbed curricula represent the thematic approach to integrating subject matter.

Example
The teacher presents a simple topical theme, such as the circus, and webs it to the subject areas. A conceptual theme, such as conflict, can be webbed for a broader thematic approach.

7   **Threaded**
Magnifying glass—big ideas that magnify all content through a metacurricular approach

Description
Standards, thinking skills, social skills, study skills, graphic organizers, technology, and a multiple intelligences approach to learning thread through all disciplines.

Example
The teaching staff targets prediction in reading, mathematics, and science lab experiments while the social studies teacher targets predicting current events, and thus threads prediction across all four disciplines.

8 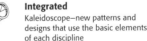 **Integrated**
Kaleidoscope—new patterns and designs that use the basic elements of each discipline

Description
The integrated curricular model represents a cross-disciplinary approach similar to the shared model.

Example
In mathematics, science, social studies, fine arts, language arts, and practical arts, teachers look for patterns and approach content through these patterns in all the discipline areas.

9  **Immersed**
Microscope—intensely personal view that allows microscopic exploration as all content is filtered through lens of interest and expertise

Description
The individual integrates all data, from every field and discipline, by funneling the ideas through his or her area of interest.

Example
A student or doctoral candidate has an area of expert interest and sees all learning through that lens.

10 **Networked**
Prism—a view that creates multiple dimensions and directions of focus

Description
The networked model of integrated learning is an ongoing external source of input, forever providing new, extended, and extrapolated or refined ideas.

Example
An architect, while adapting the CAD/CAM technology for design, networks with technical programmers and expands her knowledge base, just as she had traditionally done with interior designers.

© Robin Fogarty, 1991*

Figure 0.5   *Extrapolated from "Design Options for an Integrated Curriculum" by Heidi Hayes Jacobs in *Interdisciplinary Curriculum*, ASCD, 1989.

Ten Models of Curriculum Integration: How Are We Doing?

Are We or How Are We Integrating the Curricula?

1 **Cellular**
Are we or how are we setting curricular priorities? (How are we managing the standards?)

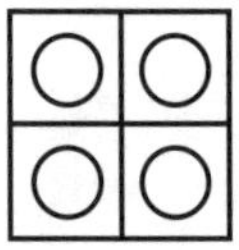

2 **Connected**
Are we or how are we connecting the curriculum in explicit ways? (How are we making connections—day to day, week to week, unit to unit?)

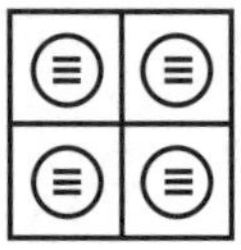

3 **Nested**
Are we or how are we explicitly nesting the life skills and process standards into a core curricular content?

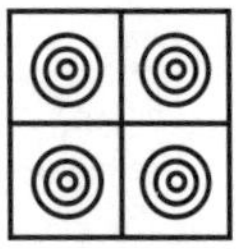

4 **Sequenced**
Are we or how are we aligning standards and mapping curriculum for commonsense parallels?

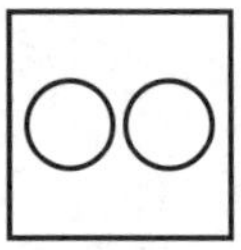

5 **Shared**
Are we or how are we collaborating with other teachers to find the big ideas that we share across the disciplines?

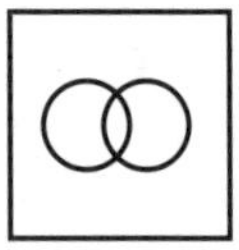

6 **Webbed**
Are we or how are we using patterns and themes to integrate the curricula?

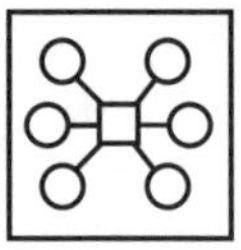

7 **Threaded**
Are we or how are we threading skills across the various content areas?

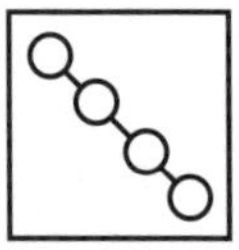

8 **Integrated**
Are we designing or how might we design authentic learning projects and performances that integrate a number of disciplines?

9 **Immersed**
Are we or how are we using learner-centered models in which students have choices?

10 **Networked**
Are we or how are we modeling real-world learning that utilizes networks of experts?

Figure 0.6

Tally Sheet for Personal Reflections and Comments

Are We or How Are We Integrating the Curricula?

1 Cellular	2 Connected
3 Nested	4 Sequenced
5 Shared	6 Webbed
7 Threaded	8 Integrated
9 Immersed	10 Networked

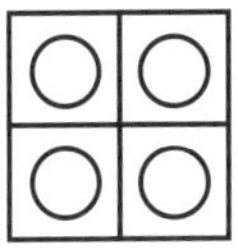

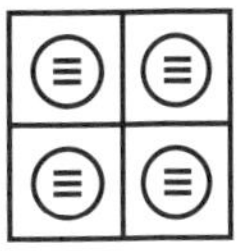

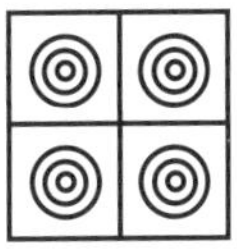

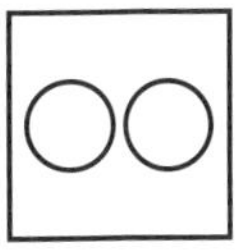

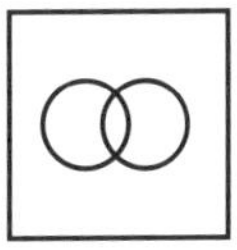

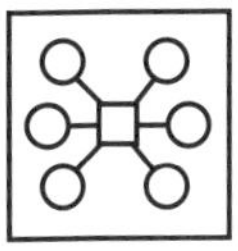

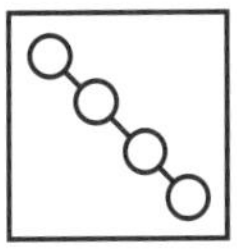

Figure 0.7

Use the Agree/Disagree chart (Figure 0.8) to record your positions regarding some statements about integrating the curricula before reading more about it.

How Do Teachers Use the Book?

The book is divided into ten chapters, one for each of the models. The discussion for each model includes answers to the following questions:

What is it?
What does it look like?
What does it sound like?
What are the advantages?
What are the disadvantages?
When is this model useful?

To complete the discussion of each model, a vignette of teachers working with the model is presented in comic book style. The scenarios depict the ongoing interactions and evolving journey of four faculty members trying to integrate the curricula.

MARIA NOVELAS

Maria Novelas, the language arts teacher, has been with the district for seventeen years, while Sue Sum is a recent graduate who landed a job in the mathematics department.

SUE SUM

BOB BEAKER

Bob Beaker has manned his science lab for the past five years, but Tom Time has been in the history department "since time began."

TOM TIME

SkyLight Professional Development

Agree/Disagree Chart (Use individual thinking first, then dialogue with a partner.)

Statement	Before		After	
	Agree	**Disagree**	**Agree**	**Disagree**
1. Integrating is connecting today's topics to yesterday's.				
2. Integrating means selecting an overall theme.				
3. Team teaching is part of integrating the curricula.				
4. It's so easy to integrate a novel with history.				
5. Math can't be integrated because it's sequential.				
6. Integrated is a synonym for inter-disciplinary.				
7. We're already doing integrated models.				
8. The purity of the discipline is lost in integrated curricula.				
9. Integrated models are easier for students, harder for teachers.				
10 Integration is clustering standards in robust projects.				
11. Integrated models take too much time.				
12. Performance tasks are examples of integrated curricula.				

Figure 0.8

CAPT. META COGNITION

In addition to the four staff members, there is Priscilla Pauley, the progressive principal who supports her teachers in their effort to more fully integrate the curricula. Also, several graduates round out the vignettes of the integrated learner models. Throughout the book, guiding comments are made by Captain Meta Cognition, our superhero, who provides a freeze-frame, metacognitive comment about the various views of curricular integration.

Following the comic strip action, each section ends with a set of graphics. These organizers are included for reader use. Each model includes actual samples of curricular integration for teachers to study and discuss. Each model also includes a graphic that requires teachers to design lessons and units using the construct.

Whether you are working alone, with partners, or in teams, the organizers provide immediate and visible transfer of the models into useful prototypes. In fact, a faculty can easily work with this over time to develop integrated curricula throughout the school. Each staff member or team can choose one model to work with each semester. As teachers begin the conversation about integrating the curricula, the spectrum of models becomes more inviting. Or, students themselves can work with the models to explore the connections they make within and across disciplines and within and across learners.

SkyLight Professional Development

Cellular

The traditional model of separate and distinct disciplines, as depicted by student learning standards in each discipline area.

CELLULAR

Periscope—one direction; one sighting; narrow focus on single discipline or content area

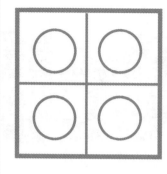

The traditional model of separate and distinct disciplines, as depicted by student learning standards in each discipline.

Example
The teacher applies this view in mathematics, science, social studies, language arts or sciences, humanities, fine and practical arts.

"Education is the instruction of the intellect in the laws of Nature."
—Thomas Huxley

What Is the Cellular Model?

The traditional curricular arrangement dictates separate and distinct disciplines. Typically, the four major academic areas are labeled mathematics, science, language arts, and social studies. Fine arts and practical arts pick up the remaining subjects of art, music, and physical education, which are sometmes considered peripheral subjects when compared to the hard-core academic areas. Another grouping of the disciplines uses the categories of humanities, sciences, practical arts, and fine arts. In the standard curriculum, these subject matter areas are taught in isolation, with no attempt to connect or integrate them. Each is seen as a pure entity in and of itself. Each has separate and distinct content standards. Although there may be overlaps in the sciences of physics and chemistry, the relationships between the two are implicitly, not explicitly, approached through the curriculum.

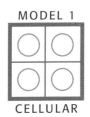

MODEL 1

CELLULAR

What Does It Look Like?

In the secondary school or junior high, each discipline is taught by different teachers in different locations throughout the building with the students moving to different rooms. Each separate encounter carries with it a separate and distinct cellular organization, leaving the student with a cellular view of the curricula. A less severe cellular model, with subjects still taught separately and apart from each other, is the elementary classroom. In this situation the teacher says, "Now, put away your math books and take out your science packets. It's time to work on our science unit." The daily schedule shows distinct time slots for mathematics, science, or social studies. Often topics from two areas are not intentionally correlated. This isolation of subjects can be the norm, even in the self-contained classroom as content standards reign supreme.

What Does It Sound Like?

A young high school student explained the traditional curriculum like a vaccination: "Math is not science; science is not English; English is not history. A subject is something you take once and need never take again. It's like getting a vaccination; I've had my shot of algebra. I'm done with that."

In one day, a typical junior high school student may be asked to perform in seven or eight very different subjects, from mathematics to physical education. The student will do this every day in addition to the homework each subject will generate. In order to cope with such a workload, students may have to choose between focusing on the one or two subjects they enjoy doing and excel in them and doing the minimum required to get by in the other subjects. Readers may wonder, "What do students learn under these circumstances?" and "Are the needs of the system taking precedence over the needs of the students?"

STUDENTS, PARENTS, AND TEACHERS—THEY'RE WONDERING HOW IT ALL FITS.

What Are the Advantages?

One of the advantages of this cellular model, of course, is that the purity of each discipline is left untainted. In addition, instructors prepare as experts in a field and have the luxury of digging into their subjects with both breadth and depth. This traditional model also provides a comfort

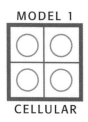

MODEL 1

CELLULAR

zone for all concerned because it represents the norm. We're used to it. The weight of these pluses must not be taken too lightly. There is value in examining one discipline or subject as a separate and distinct entity in order to reveal the critical attributes of each discrete field. This model, although somewhat fragmented, does provide clear and discrete views of the disciplines. Experts can easily sift out the priorities of their own subject areas. Also, students realize the benefits of working with a mentor in this model.

What Are the Disadvantages?

The disadvantages are twofold. Learners are left to their own resources to make connections or integrate similar concepts. In addition, overlapping concepts, skills, and attitudes are not illuminated for the learner and transfer of learning to novel situations is less likely to occur. To leave the learner unattended in making connections both within and across the disciplines is to overlook some of the latest research on transfer of learning, which calls for explicit bridging. Also, in this discipline-based model, students can easily get caught in an avalanche of work. Although each teacher assigns a reasonable amount, the cumulative effect can become overwhelming for the students.

When Is This Cellular Model Useful?

This is a useful curricular configuration for large schools with diverse populations because these schools may offer a variety of courses that provide a spectrum of subjects that target special interests. It is most useful at the university level where students travel on specialized paths of study that require expert knowledge for instructing, mentoring, coaching, and collaborating. Even before the university level, this model is helpful to teachers, whose preparation can be more focused. It is also a good model for teachers who want to sift out curricular priorities in order to manage the abundance of content standards as they prepare cross-departmental models for interdisciplinary planning. Figure 1.1 is an example of completed cellular models of integration, and Figure 1.2 provides the opportunity for readers to record their own designs for this model.

LET'S NOT DISMISS THE TRADITIONAL MODEL TOO LIGHTLY. IT'S WORKED FOR MANY YEARS. THERE MUST BE A REASON IT HAS SURVIVED THE TEST OF TIME.

MARIA NOVELAS-LANGUAGE ARTS
STUDENTS CAN RENT THE MOVIE *ROMEO AND JULIET* OVER THE WEEKEND. THEY WILL BE FAMILIAR WITH THE PLOT AND WE CAN FOCUS ON THE BEAUTY OF SHAKESPEAREAN ENGLISH ON MONDAY.

MEANWHILE, BACK AT THE SCHOOL, TEACHERS WITH PERISCOPIC VISION ARE UNINTENTIONALLY BURYING THEIR STUDENTS WITH HOMEWORK AS THEY INDIVIDUALLY PLAN THEIR CURRICULA . . .

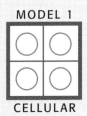

MODEL 1

CELLULAR

TOM TIME-HISTORY
THIS LIST OF TOPICS WILL HELP STUDENTS SELECT THEIR SEMESTER PROJECTS ON WESTERN CIVILIZATION. THEY CAN START RESEARCHING THEIR PROJECTS THIS WEEKEND.

SUE SUM-MATHEMATICS
IF WE GET THROUGH THIS LESSON TODAY, I'LL ASSIGN THESE THEOREMS FOR WEEK-END HOMEWORK.

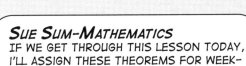

BOB BEAKER-SCIENCE
STUDENTS CAN READ THE CHAPTER ON THE PERIODIC TABLE OF ELEMENTS OVER THE WEEKEND. IT'S LONG, BUT THEN THEY'LL HAVE A JUMP ON THE REST OF THE SEMESTER.

FOUR SAMPLES FOR CELLULAR MODELS

MODEL 1

CELLULAR

Individually, list the curriculum pieces by content areas or by preparatory subjects (algebra, geometry, trigonometry) and then prioritize the list. Then, dialogue with a partner in the same department or similar grade level about the curricular priorities in that discipline. Discuss how you set priorities and what you considered in making decisions about how to weigh things in the curriculum.

Mathematics

List	Rank
✓ Logic/Reasoning	2
✓ Problem Solving	1
✓ Technology Use	6
✓ Estimation	3
✓ Geometry Concepts	4
✓ Algebraic Concepts	5

Science

List	Rank
✓ Research	2
✓ Systems	3
✓ Change/Evolution	4
✓ Cause/Effect	5
✓ Structure/Function	6
✓ Experimentation/ Discovery	1

Language Arts

List	Rank
✓ Grammar	6
✓ Research	4
✓ Genre Study	3
✓ Writing: The Essay	2
✓ Communications	5
✓ Critical Analysis	1

Social Studies

List	Rank
✓ Map Skills	5
✓ Population/Environment	2
✓ Geographical Features	6
✓ Social Systems	1
✓ Economic Systems	4
✓ Conflict Resolution	3

NOTES & REFLECTIONS

Each discipline plans its topics and content in isolation from the other disciplines. For example, the Language Arts teacher lists the typical topics for a semester. The sequence and time allotment is determined by the individual teacher using individual criteria while sifting out curricular priorities; "selectively abandoning"* or "judiciously including"* material in curricular designing.

(*Costa 1991a)

Figure 1.1

DESIGN FOR CELLULAR MODEL

MODEL 1

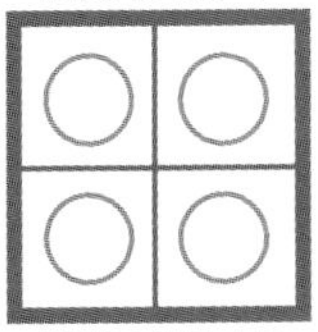

CELLULAR

Individually, list the curriculum pieces by content areas or by preparatory subjects (algebra, geometry, trigonometry) and then prioritize the list. Then, dialogue with a partner in the same department or similar grade level about the curricular priorities in that discipline. Discuss how you set priorities and what you considered in making decisions about how to weigh things in the curriculum.

List _____ Rank
✔ _____ ☐
✔ _____ ☐
✔ _____ ☐
✔ _____ ☐
✔ _____ ☐
✔ _____ ☐

List _____ Rank
✔ _____ ☐
✔ _____ ☐
✔ _____ ☐
✔ _____ ☐
✔ _____ ☐
✔ _____ ☐

List _____ Rank
✔ _____ ☐
✔ _____ ☐
✔ _____ ☐
✔ _____ ☐
✔ _____ ☐
✔ _____ ☐

List _____ Rank
✔ _____ ☐
✔ _____ ☐
✔ _____ ☐
✔ _____ ☐
✔ _____ ☐
✔ _____ ☐

NOTES & REFLECTIONS

List some criteria that helped you set curricular priorities.

Figure 1.2

Connected

MODEL

2

Within each subject area, course content is
connected topic to topic, concept to concept,
one year's work to the next, and relates
ideas explicitly.

C O N N E C T E D

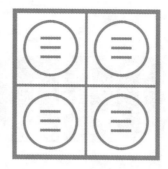

Within each subject area, course content is connected topic to topic, concept to concept, one year's work to the next, and relates ideas explicitly.

Opera glass—details of one discipline; focus on subtleties and interconnections

Example
The teacher relates the concept of fractions to decimals, which in turn relates to money, grades, etc.

"The object of education is to prepare the young to educate themselves throughout their lives."—Robert Maynard Hutchins

What Is the Connected Model?

Although the major discipline areas remain separate, this curricular model focuses on making explicit connections within each subject area, connecting one topic to the next, connecting one concept to another, connecting a skill to a related skill, connecting one day's work to the next, or even connecting one semester's ideas to the next. The key to this model is the effort to deliberately relate curricula within the discipline rather than assuming that students understand the connections automatically. In this way, students are aware of the flow of content created by the teacher. This flow enhances the connectivity between the various topics presented.

What Does It Look Like?

Within the elementary curriculum, for example, a relationship is drawn between the rock unit and the simple machines unit as students explicitly connect these while simultaneously seeing them as two distinct science areas: one is Earth science and the other is physical science—both considered part of the sciences per se. By labeling for students the broad terms (in this case, Earth science and physical science), students can begin to define the sciences for themselves by using these as organizational umbrellas. This becomes a first critical step in their understanding and conceptualizing the sciences as a realm of knowing.

MODEL 2

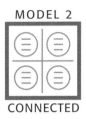

CONNECTED

Likewise, in a middle or secondary school setting, the Earth science teacher relates the geology unit to the astronomy unit by associating the evolutionary nature of each. The similarities between the two units become organizers for students as they work through both units to see that they can make explicit interrelationships.

What Does It Sound Like?

The student sees connections between subject areas that have traditionally been taught separately. For example, a student concludes that a particular law in physics has logical inconsistencies. Then, he notices that when he looks at biology, he encounters that law again, but again, finds logical contradictions. By looking across disciplines, he finds specific examples that he connects to support his thoughts about that particular law. The teacher can facilitate such connections in students' thinking by explicitly making links between subject areas.

TEACHERS CAN HELP STUDENTS MAKE CONNECTIONS BY ASKING QUESTIONS THAT STRETCH IDEAS.

What Are the Advantages?

By connecting ideas within a discipline, the learner has the advantage of the big picture as well as a focused study of one aspect. In addition, key concepts are developed over time for internalization by the learner. Connecting ideas within a discipline permits the learner to review, reconceptualize, edit, and assimilate ideas gradually and may facilitate transfer.

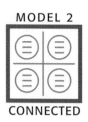

MODEL 2

CONNECTED

What Are the Disadvantages?

The various disciplines in this model remain separated and appear unrelated, yet connections are made explicit *within* the designated discipline. Teachers are not encouraged to work together in this model, so content remains the focus without stretching concepts and ideas across other disciplines. The concentrated efforts to integrate within the discipline overlook opportunities to develop more global relationships to other subjects.

When Is This Connected Model Useful?

The connected model is useful as a beginning step toward an integrated curriculum. Teachers feel confident looking for connections within their own discipline. As they become adept at relating ideas within the discipline, it becomes easier to scout for connections across disciplines. This process of connecting ideas applies to the content standards also. It is one way teachers manage and make sense of the overwhelming number of standards. Also, connection making can be done collaboratively within department meetings—which is, again, old and familiar ground that sets a safe climate for change. Starting teacher teams using this model within the department or grade level can be a fruitful strategy to prime the pump for more complex integration models later on.

Figure 2.1 is an example of completed connected models of integration and Figure 2.2 provides the opportunity for readers to try their own design for this model.

MODEL 2

CONNECTED

I WANT TO PRESENT UNITS SO THEY MAKE MORE SENSE TO THE STUDENTS. IT SEEMS LOGICAL TO INTRODUCE THE CONCEPT OF NEGATIVE NUMBERS AFTER THEY WORK WITH THE QUADRANTS IN GRAPHING.

BACK AT SCHOOL, OUR TEACHERS START TO EXPLORE THE *CONNECTORS* WITHIN THEIR OWN SUBJECT AREAS.

TO HELP STUDENTS UNDERSTAND HOW EVERYTHING IN BIOLOGY IS RELATED TO THE THEORY OF EVOLUTION, I'LL HAVE THEM KEEP AN "EVOLUTION" NOTEBOOK. THEY CAN LOG IDEAS AS WE STUDY, READ, AND DISCUSS VARIOUS TOPICS.

TO GENERATE AN INTEGRATED UNDERSTANDING OF AMERICAN LITERATURE, I'LL ASK STUDENTS TO CRITIQUE EACH AUTHOR WE READ THIS SEMESTER USING "THE AMERICAN DREAM" AS A THEME. THIS WILL WEAVE A COMMON STRAND THROUGHOUT THE UNITS.

BY INTERTWINING THE UNIT ON EARLY GREECE WITH GREEK DRAMA, STUDENTS WILL GET A STUDY OF HUMANITIES RATHER THAN DISCRETE STUDIES OF HISTORY AND LITERATURE. IT SHOULD PROVIDE A MORE ENDURING IMAGE OF THE ERA.

FOUR SAMPLES FOR CONNECTED MODELS

MODEL 2

CONNECTED

Think of two units, topics, or concepts within a discipline or class you teach. Put one on the top line and another on the bottom line to represent sequence. One is taught before the other. Now, think about why you put them together that way. Jot down on the center line the connecting ideas—the concepts, skills, or attitudes that help you make your sequence a logical flow of ideas.

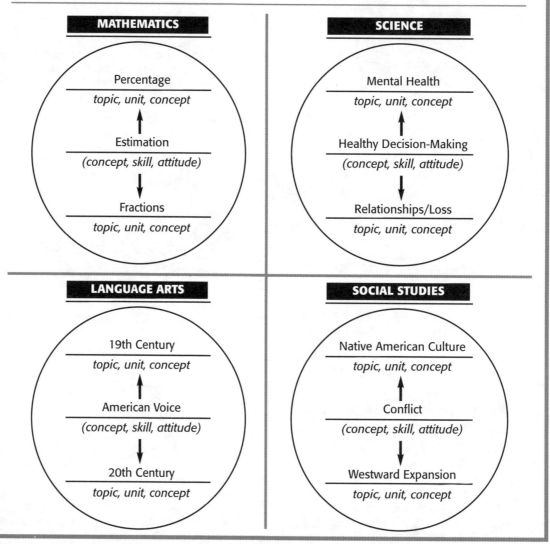

NOTES & REFLECTIONS

Each discipline connects particular topics, units, or concepts with connecting organizers. These frameworks provide common focal points for integrating idea.

Figure 2.1

FOUR DESIGNS FOR CONNECTED MODELS

MODEL 2

CONNECTED

Think of two units, topics, or concepts within a discipline or class you teach. Put one on the top line and another on the bottom line to represent sequence. One is taught before the other. Now, think about why you put them together that way. Jot down on the center line the connecting ideas—the concepts, skills, or attitudes that help you make your sequence a logical flow of ideas.

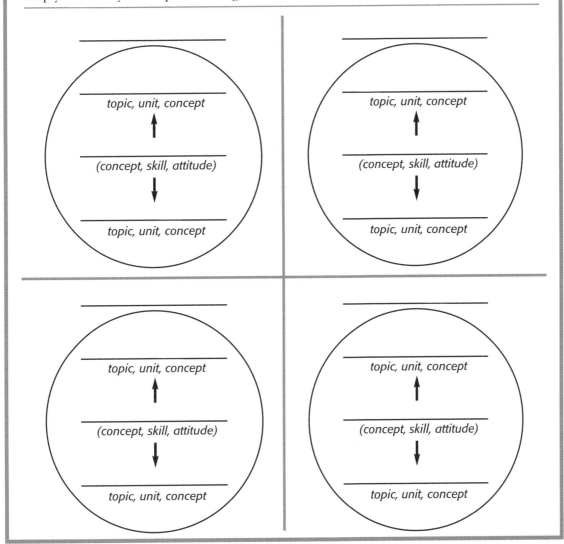

NOTES & REFLECTIONS

Figure 2.2

Nested

Within each subject area, the teacher targets
multiple skills: a social skill, a thinking skill,
and a content-specific skill based on standards.

N E S T E D

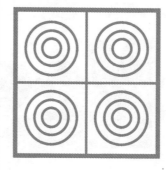

Within each subject area, the teacher targets multiple skills: a social skill, a thinking skill, and a content-specific skill based on standards.

3-D glasses—multiple dimensions to one scene, topic, or unit.

Example
The teacher designs the unit on photosynthesis to simultaneously target consensus seeking (social skill), sequencing (thinking skill), and plant life cycle (science content).

"The business of education is not to make the young perfect in any one of the sciences, but to open and dispose their minds as may best make them capable of any, when they shall apply themselves to it."—John Locke

What Is the Nested Model?

The nested model of integration is a rich design used by skilled teachers. They know how to get the most mileage from the lesson—any lesson. But, in this nested approach to instruction, careful planning is needed to structure multiple targets and multiple standards for student learning. However, nested integration takes advantage of natural clusters and combinations so the task seems pretty easy.

What Does It Look Like?

An elementary content lesson on the circulatory system targets the concept of systems as well as facts and understanding on the circulatory system in particular. But, in addition to this conceptual target, the teacher also targets a thinking skill or a process standard such as cause and effect. Throughout the study of the circulatory system, students will be focusing on causes and effects as they pertain to the circulatory system.

In addition, a social skill such as cooperation may be a focal point as the class learns about group work. Also, flow-chart design may be an organizational skill developed during this unit. So, as the teacher covers the content standards, generic, generalized life skills are nested together to enhance the learning experience. Some examples of skills that may be targeted for nesting are shown in Figure 3.1.

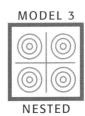

MODEL 3

NESTED

THINKING SKILLS	SOCIAL SKILLS	STANDARDS	GRAPHIC ORGANIZERS
• predicting • inferring • comparing/contrasting • classifying • generalizing • hypothesizing • prioritizing • visualizing	• attentive listening • clarifying • paraphrasing • encouraging • accepting ideas • disagreeing • consensus seeking • summarizing	• science standard: inquiry • math standard: analysis of data • history standard: democratic process • language arts standard: expository writing • art standard: appreciation of art forms	• web • Venn • flowchart • mind map • fishbone • matrix

Figure 3.1

A high school lesson in a computer science class may target the Computer Assisted Drawing/Computer Assisted Manufacturing (CAD/CAM) programs. Yet, as the students learn the actual workings of the program, the teacher also targets the thinking skill of visualizing for explicit exploration and practice. In this nested approach, students are also instructed in ergonomics as they design furniture for schools of the future. Thus, the teacher clusters several skills and/or process standards in this nested model of integrating the curricula.

WHEN YOU THINK ABOUT IT, ANY LESSON CAN BE SET UP TO INCORPORATE THE NESTED MODEL.

What Does It Sound Like?

STUDENT 1: Teachers used to be pretty predictable. They would tell you what you were supposed to know and they tested you on it.

STUDENT 2: Yeah! I know what you mean. It was easy to psych out the test questions because the stuff was repeated eighteen times in class.

STUDENT 1: But now, they expect you to sort out what's important. And they want you to tell them how you figure things out.

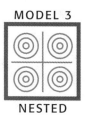

MODEL 3

NESTED

STUDENT 2: That's not all. My teacher watches our social behavior, too. She says our thinking and our behavior are just as important as our answers. This is getting out of control.

STUDENT 1: Yeah! They're getting too much mileage out of one lousy lesson.

What Are the Advantages?

The pluses of the nested model are obvious to the veteran teacher. By nesting and clustering a number of skills and standards in the learning experience, student learning is enriched and enhanced. Typically, focusing on content, thinking strategies, social skills, and other serendipitous ideas, the single lesson takes on multiple dimensions. In this day and age of information overload, overcrowded curricula, numerous standards, and tight schedules, the experienced teacher may seek out fertile lessons that lay the groundwork for learning in multiple areas. While the nested model provides the needed attention to several areas of interest at once, it does not require the added burden of finding time to work and plan with another teacher. With this model, a single teacher can provide extensive integration of curricula.

What Are the Disadvantages?

The possible disadvantages of the nested model arise from its very nature. Nesting two, three, or four learning targets and/or standards into a single lesson may confuse students if the nesting is not executed carefully. The conceptual priorities of the lesson may become obscure because students are directed to perform many learning tasks at once.

When Is This Nested Model Useful?

The nested model is most appropriate to use as teachers try to infuse the process standards, such as thinking skills, cooperative skills, and literacy skills, into their content lessons. Keeping the content objectives in place while adding a thinking focus, targeting social skills, and infusing literacy skills enhances the overall learning experience. Nesting particular skills in these three areas integrates concepts and attitudes easily through structured activities. Figure 3.2 is an example of completed nested models of integration, and Figure 3.3 provides the opportunity for readers to record their own designs for this model.

MEANWHILE, BACK AT SCHOOL, OUR TEACHERS ARE GETTING A LOT OF MILEAGE OUT OF THEIR LESSONS— THEY'RE TARGETING SOCIAL SKILLS, THINKING SKILLS, *AND* CONTENT SKILLS *WITHIN* A SINGLE LESSON.

I LIKE THE IDEA OF "NESTED" SKILLS AS A WAY TO INTEGRATE. IT KEEPS MY DISCIPLINE PURE AND INTACT, YET I EXTEND THE LESSON INTO OTHER REALMS. IN GLOBAL STUDIES, I CAN USE DE BONO'S *SIX THINKING HATS* FOR POINT OF VIEW OF CURRENT EVENTS. WITH A JIGSAW MODEL, I CAN TALK ABOUT STUDENT RESPONSIBILITY.

MODEL 3

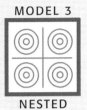

NESTED

GOOD IDEA, TOM! WHEN I INTRODUCE THE PERIODIC TABLE OF ELEMENTS, I COULD FOCUS ON THE CONTENT OF THE CHART, AND THEN TRY NESTING OTHER SKILLS AND CONCEPTS SUCH AS PATTERNS OR MEMORY TECHNIQUES.

WHILE TEACHING *THE OLD MAN AND THE SEA,* I CAN FOCUS ON AUTHOR STYLE AND USE OF LANGUAGE AS I HAVE IN THE PAST. BUT I CAN ALSO TARGET THE CONCEPTS OF PERSEVERANCE AND FRIENDSHIP. EMPHASIZING TEAMWORK AS A SOCIAL SKILL LOOKS POSSIBLE.

IN A MATH LESSON, I CAN TEACH THE SKILL OF GRAPHING INFORMATION AND ALSO EMPHASIZE PREDICTION OF THE LINE. I COULD USE THE IDEA OF NESTING, AND REQUIRE CONSENSUS IN THE GROUP FOR PREDICTIONS.

FOUR SAMPLES FOR NESTED MODELS

MODEL 3

NESTED

Target a content standard that carries a lot of weight in your curriculum. Then, add at least two outer circles, and nest in several process standards to illustrate graphically how you are able to layer, cluster, and combine a number of standards into a robust learning experience.

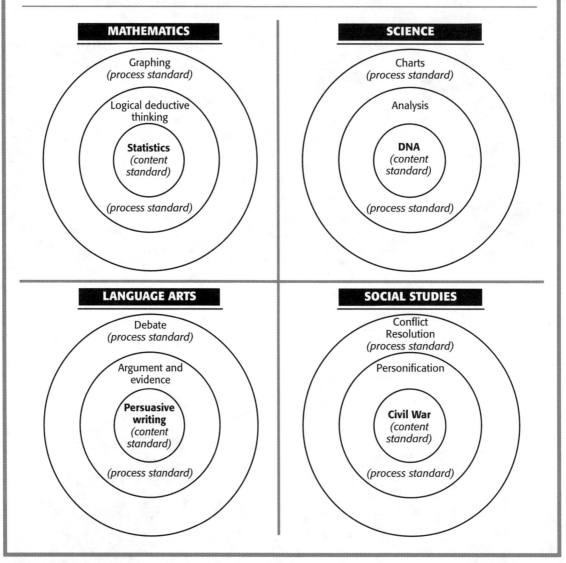

MATHEMATICS

Graphing
(process standard)

Logical deductive
thinking

Statistics
*(content
standard)*

(process standard)

SCIENCE

Charts
(process standard)

Analysis

DNA
*(content
standard)*

(process standard)

LANGUAGE ARTS

Debate
(process standard)

Argument and
evidence

**Persuasive
writing**
*(content
standard)*

(process standard)

SOCIAL STUDIES

Conflict
Resolution
(process standard)

Personification

Civil War
*(content
standard)*

(process standard)

NOTES & REFLECTIONS

Within a content standard, the teacher uses the subject matter as the frame for a number of skills, concepts, and attitudes. The topic or unit provides the vehicle to carry along learning in related areas.

Figure 3.2

SkyLight Professional Development

FOUR DESIGNS FOR NESTED MODELS

MODEL 3

NESTED

Target a content standard that carries a lot of weight in your curriculum. Then, add at least two outer circles, and nest in several process standards to illustrate graphically how you are able to layer, cluster, and combine a number of standards into a robust learning experience.

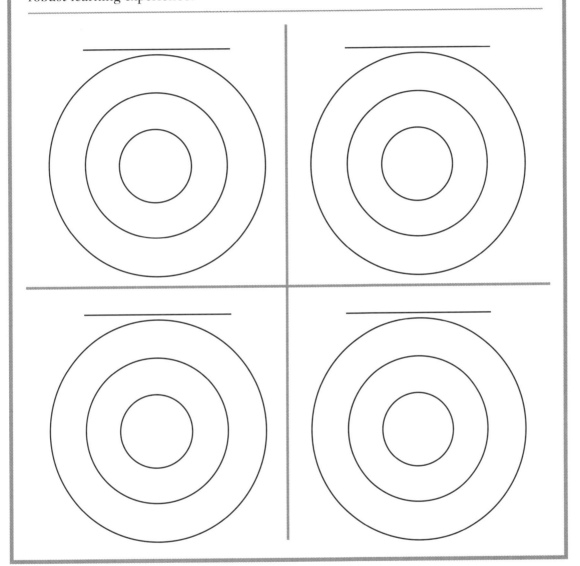

NOTES & REFLECTIONS

Figure 3.3

Sequenced

HOW ARE WE ALIGNING STANDARDS AND MAPPING CURRICULUM FOR COM-MONSENSE PARALLELS?

Topics or units of study are rearranged and
sequenced to coincide with one another.
Similar ideas are taught in concert while
remaining separate subjects.

SEQUENCED

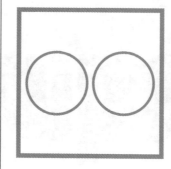

Topics or units of study are rearranged and sequenced to coincide with one another. Similar ideas are taught in concert while remaining separate subjects.

Eyeglasses—varied internal content framed by broad, related topics

Example
An English teacher presents a historical novel depicting a particular period while the history teacher teaches that same historical period.

"Education is the transmission of civilization."
—Will and Ariel Durant

What Is the Sequenced Model?

With limited articulation across disciplines, teachers can rearrange the order of their topics so that similar units coincide with each other. Two related disciplines may be sequenced so that the subject matter content of both are taught in parallel. By sequencing the order in which topics are taught, the activities of each enhance the other. In essence, one subject carries the other and vice versa.

If a district or school has not done any curriculum mapping, this model provides a tool to begin the process. If the district or school has done some curriculum mapping by grade level or department, the next step is to begin the conversation across two subject areas that seem most likely to have connections. Or, a teacher may match up with a friend and colleague in the building and try mapping and resequencing some topics or units that seem natural mates. This facilitates connection making for the learners in both subject areas and reinforces learning as it enhances the two curricular topics under study.

SkyLight Professional Development

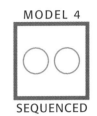

MODEL 4

SEQUENCED

What Does It Look Like?

In the self-contained classroom, *Charlotte's Web* can accompany the unit on spiders. *Johnny Tremain* can parallel the study of the Revolutionary War. The graphing unit can coincide with data collection in the weather unit.

A secondary situation might sequence the study of the stock market in mathematics with the study of the Depression in history. Both domestic and global events can be used to parallel various units in the various subjects. In this way, current, relevant topics become the catalyst to study historic foundations, related mathematical concepts, or appropriate literary references.

What Does It Sound Like?

John Adams once said, "The textbook is not a moral contract that teachers are obliged to teach—teachers are obliged to teach children." Unfortunately, more often than one cares to admit, teachers may follow the format of the texts, going from the front of the book to the back, or they try to teach each standard separately. Although this may work well in some cases, it might make more sense to rearrange the sequence of the units in other cases. The new sequence may be more logical if it parallels subject matter content across disciplines. When learners are given the advantage of seeing these natural connections across content, both the students and the teachers benefit. Learning becomes more generalized and therefore more easily transferred.

JUST BY REARRANGING THE ORDER OF TOPICS, TEACHERS CAN HELP KIDS MAKE THOSE CRITICAL CONNECTIONS.

What Are the Advantages?

The teacher, by rearranging the sequence of topics, chapters, and units, can dictate the curricular priorities rather than follow the sequence established by the editorial staff of the textbook. In this way, teachers can make the critical decisions about content. From the students' point of view, the deliberate sequencing of related topics across disciplines helps them make sense of their studies in both subject and content areas. Once again, integration aids transfer. When students see teachers in different content areas, in different rooms, in different periods, making similar points, their learning is reinforced in a powerful and meaningful way.

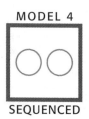

MODEL 4

SEQUENCED

What Are the Disadvantages?

A drawback of sequenced curricula is the compromise required to shape the model. Teachers must give up autonomy in making curriculum sequences as they partner with others. Also, to sequence according to current events requires ongoing collaboration and extreme flexibility on the part of all content-area people involved. This is not as easy as it sounds. However, in a very short time, even with only one afternoon together, teacher partners can easily do some rearranging and sequencing as a beginning step. If this first attempt at correlating two subject areas works, the two teachers can try sequencing more units for parallel teaching.

When Is This Sequenced Model Useful?

The sequenced model is useful in the beginning stages of the integration process, using two discipline areas that are easily tied to each other. The teacher, working with a partner, starts by listing curricular content separately. Then, the team juggles the separate content pieces until the two can match up or sequence some things to coincide. They try to parallel their different contents to make more sense to the students who are learning both. In this model, both disciplines stay pure. Specific emphasis is still in the domain of the subject matter, but the student reaps the benefits of related content.

In addition, the sequenced model is useful, as mentioned earlier, to begin the conversations across disciplines and across subject areas. In elementary schools, classroom teachers can work the sequenced model with special area teachers. The regular education teachers can work with the music teacher, the art teacher, the physical education teacher, or special educators, such as the reading teacher or the learning disabilities teacher.

At the middle and high school levels, of course, teachers can reach across two content areas and see what happens. The conversation is as important as the final product in a pairing such as this, because in the conversation teachers learn about other teachers' content. Once aware, it is easy to make connections to those subject areas to help students see the cohesiveness.

Figures 4.1, 4.2, and 4.3 are examples of completed sequenced integration exercises, and Figure 4.4 provides the opportunity for readers to record their own design for this model.

SkyLight Professional Development

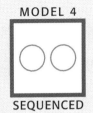

MODEL 4

SEQUENCED

BY NOW, TEACHERS AT SCHOOL ARE BEGINNING TO SEE THE ADVANTAGES OF MAKING CONNECTIONS FOR BOTH LESSONS AND LEARNERS. OUR TEACHERS START TALKING ABOUT DOING SOME PLANNING *TOGETHER*.

AS WE AGREED IN OUR LAST FACULTY MEETING, BOB, I'VE LISTED THE KEY UNITS I WILL COVER THIS SEMESTER IN THE USUAL ORDER.

GREAT, SUE! I DID A SIMILAR LIST. LET'S COMPARE LISTS AND SEE IF THERE'S A LOGICAL SEQUENCING SO THE UNITS HAVE MORE MATCH UP FOR STUDENTS.

SOUNDS GOOD. IT WOULD BE EASY FOR ME TO ADJUST AND I LIKE THE IDEA OF REINFORCEMENT OF THE CONCEPTS IN MATH CLASS.

TEACHER'S LOUNGE

I'VE NOTICED YOU'VE LISTED YOUR UNIT ON POLLUTION. I TEACH A SIMILAR LITERATURE UNIT ON PROJECTING FUTURE PROBLEMS. MAYBE WE COULD PLAN SOME FILMS OR FIELD EXPERIENCES TOGETHER.

YOU KNOW, MARIA, THAT MAKES A LOT OF SENSE. I'M GLAD WE STARTED LOOKING AT ALL OF THIS. IT'S REFRESHING TO JUGGLE THINGS AROUND SOMETIMES.

MODEL 4

○ ○

SEQUENCED

SAMPLE FOR SEQUENCED MODEL: TWO SUBJECTS

Working with two different subject areas, teachers list their topics or units by the month on the lines at the bottom of the page, giving a long look at the term. Then, after listing topics on the lines, they try to find one or two parallel units to list in the circles.

LANGUAGE ARTS
subject

Sequence
1. *Robin Hood*
2. *The Midnight Ride of Paul Revere*
3. *The Slave Who Bought His Freedom*
4. *Nellie Bly*
5. *Diary of Anne Frank*
6. Newspaper
7. Persuasive Writing
8. Research Paper
9. Debate
10. Poetry

List
- ✓ Sept.–*Robin Hood*
- ✓ Oct.–*Nellie Bly*
- ✓ Nov.–*Diary of Anne Frank*
- ✓ Dec.–*The Midnight Ride of Paul Revere*
- ✓ Jan.–*The Slave Who Bought His Freedom*
- ✓ Feb.–Research Paper
- ✓ Mar.–Persuasive Writing
- ✓ Apr.–Debate
- ✓ May–Poetry
- ✓ June–Newspaper

SOCIAL STUDIES
subject

Sequence
1. Medieval times
2. American Revolution
3. Civil War
4. Women's Suffrage Movement
5. World War II
6. Depression
7. "Best" Decade
8. Region Report
9. Industrial Revolution
10. West

List
- ✓ Sept.–Amer. Hist.–Region Report
- ✓ Oct.–Amer. Hist.–Civil War
- ✓ Nov.–Amer. Hist.–Women's Suffrage
- ✓ Dec.–World Hist.–Medieval Times
- ✓ Jan.–World War II
- ✓ Feb.–World Hist.–Region Report
- ✓ Mar.–Amer. Hist.–Westward Movement
- ✓ Apr.–Amer. Hist.–Industrial Revolution
- ✓ May–Amer. Hist.–Decades
- ✓ June–Amer. Hist.–Depression

NOTES & REFLECTIONS

Sequencing units with another teacher is an easy way to ensure that students make connections.

Figure 4.1

SAMPLE FOR SEQUENCED MODEL: ONE YEAR

MODEL 4

SEQUENCED

Working with two different subject areas, begin with one teacher talking and writing the list of topics or units by the month, giving a long look at the term. Then, the second teacher does the same. After listing the topics on the lines, try to find parallel units to list in the circles. Sometimes, there are many parallel units, and other times there are only one or two that make sense. Just begin the conversation and see what happens.

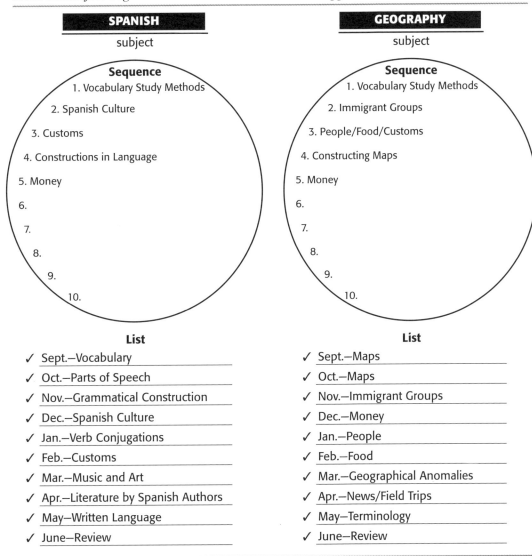

SPANISH
subject

Sequence
1. Vocabulary Study Methods
2. Spanish Culture
3. Customs
4. Constructions in Language
5. Money
6.
7.
8.
9.
10.

List
✓ Sept.–Vocabulary
✓ Oct.–Parts of Speech
✓ Nov.–Grammatical Construction
✓ Dec.–Spanish Culture
✓ Jan.–Verb Conjugations
✓ Feb.–Customs
✓ Mar.–Music and Art
✓ Apr.–Literature by Spanish Authors
✓ May–Written Language
✓ June–Review

GEOGRAPHY
subject

Sequence
1. Vocabulary Study Methods
2. Immigrant Groups
3. People/Food/Customs
4. Constructing Maps
5. Money
6.
7.
8.
9.
10.

List
✓ Sept.–Maps
✓ Oct.–Maps
✓ Nov.–Immigrant Groups
✓ Dec.–Money
✓ Jan.–People
✓ Feb.–Food
✓ Mar.–Geographical Anomalies
✓ Apr.–News/Field Trips
✓ May–Terminology
✓ June–Review

NOTES & REFLECTIONS

Figure 4.2

MODEL 4

SEQUENCED

SAMPLE FOR SEQUENCED MODEL: ONE SEMESTER

Working with two different subject areas, begin with one teacher talking and writing the list of topics or units by the month, giving a long look at the term. Then, the second teacher does the same. After listing the topics on the lines, try to find parallel units to list in the circles. Sometimes, there are many parallel units, and other times there are only one, two, or maybe none that make sense. Just begin the conversation and see what happens.

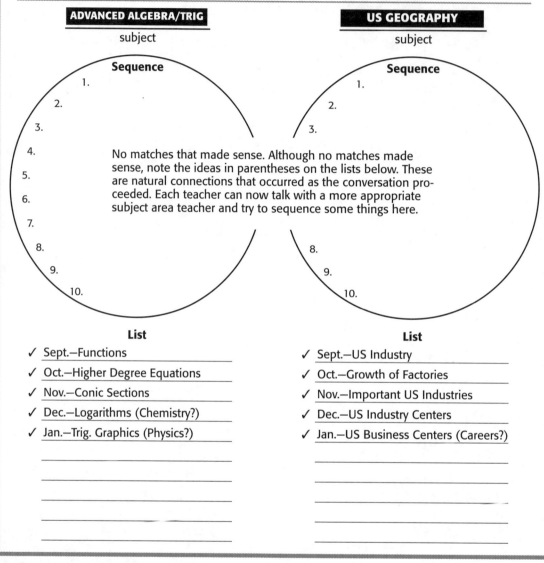

ADVANCED ALGEBRA/TRIG
subject

Sequence
1.
2.
3.
4.
5.
6.
7.
8.
9.
10.

US GEOGRAPHY
subject

Sequence
1.
2.
3.

No matches that made sense. Although no matches made sense, note the ideas in parentheses on the lists below. These are natural connections that occurred as the conversation proceeded. Each teacher can now talk with a more appropriate subject area teacher and try to sequence some things here.

8.
9.
10.

List
✓ Sept.—Functions
✓ Oct.—Higher Degree Equations
✓ Nov.—Conic Sections
✓ Dec.—Logarithms (Chemistry?)
✓ Jan.—Trig. Graphics (Physics?)

List
✓ Sept.—US Industry
✓ Oct.—Growth of Factories
✓ Nov.—Important US Industries
✓ Dec.—US Industry Centers
✓ Jan.—US Business Centers (Careers?)

NOTES & REFLECTIONS

Figure 4.3

DESIGN FOR SEQUENCED MODEL

MODEL 4

SEQUENCED

Working with two different subject areas, begin with one teacher talking and writing the list of topics or units by the month, giving a long look at the term. Then, the second teacher does the same. After listing the topics on the lines, try to find parallel units to list in the circles. Sometimes, there are many parallel units, and other times there are only one or two, or maybe none, that make sense. Just begin the conversation and see what happens.

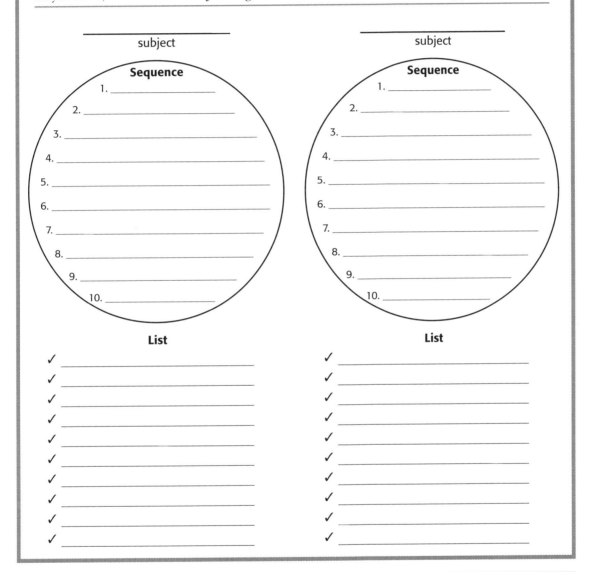

NOTES & REFLECTIONS

Figure 4.4

Shared

Shared planning takes place in two
disciplines in which overlapping concepts or
ideas emerge as organizing elements.

S H A R E D

Binoculars—two disciplines that share overlapping concepts and skills

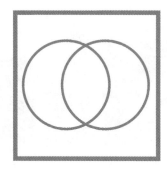

Shared planning takes place in two disciplines in which overlapping concepts or ideas emerge as organizing elements.

Example
Science and mathematics teachers use data collection, charting, and graphing as shared concepts.

"The chief object of education is not to learn things, but to unlearn things."—G. K. Chesterton

What Is the Shared Model?

Certain broad disciplines create encompassing curricular umbrellas: mathematics and science paired as sciences; language arts and history coupled under the label of the humanities; art, music, dance, and drama viewed as the fine arts; and computer technology, industrial arts, and home arts embraced as the practical arts. Within these complementary disciplines, partner planning and/or teaching create a focus on shared concepts, skills, and attitudes.

What Does It Look Like?

Cross-departmental or cross-subject area teachers partner to plan an in-depth unit of study in the elementary, middle, or high school. The two members of the team approach the preliminary planning session with a notion of key concepts, skills, and attitudes traditionally taught within the single subject approach. As the pair identify their respective priorities, they look for overlaps in subject matter content. For example, the literature teacher may focus on the concept of "the American

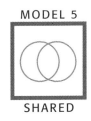

MODEL 5

SHARED

dream" as an organizer for a collection of short stories by American authors. At the same time, the history teacher notes that the unit on American history, which focuses on a study of each of the decades, could also use "the American dream" as a unifying theme.

The shared curricula model is based on shared ideas that come from within the disciplines. This model differs radically from the thematic approach in the conceptualization of the unifying concepts because the concepts result from shared elements rather than the introduction of a theme from the outside. (The shared model is an inductive approach, whereas the webbed or thematic model uses a deductive approach.) This is what a Venn diagram, shown in Figure 5.1, represents—similarities in the overlapped section. The key is to look for concepts, topics, skills, attitudes, standards, and habits of mind that occur in both subjects.

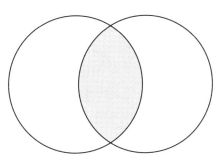

Figure 5.1

To use the shared view of curricular integration, the teacher needs to explore two disciplines for mutual concepts, skills, and/or attitudes as well as for actual content overlaps. This process is more complex than simply sequencing units to coincide with another subject area. Rather than using a long look at the semester or year, teachers go in-depth with two units of study.

What Does It Sound Like?

Elementary models of shared curricula embody standard planning models already in wide use. The self-contained classroom teacher plans the science unit on simple machines and the social studies unit on the Industrial Revolution around the concept of efficiency models. The shared concept of efficiency becomes the organizing umbrella. When using this model, teachers ask each other questions such as the following: What concepts do these units share? Are we

MODEL 5

SHARED

teaching similar skills? Do the two units have shared ideas in terms of concepts, skills, attitudes, and standards?

What Are the Advantages?

Advantages of this model of shared curriculum planning rest in its easy use as an early step toward more fully integrated models that encompass the four major disciplines. By coupling similar disciplines, the overlaps facilitate deep learning of concepts for transfer. Simply put, it's easier to schedule common planning periods for a two-teacher team than it is to juggle the scheduling for a four-teacher team. In addition, planning often leads to shared instructional experiences, such as a film or field trip, because the two teachers may be able to put their two periods back to back, or together, to create a larger time block.

What Are the Disadvantages?

A barrier to shared curricula is the planning time needed to develop the models. In addition to the time, flexibility and compromise are essential ingredients for successful implementation—it requires both trust and teamwork. This model of integration across two disciplines requires commitment from the partners to work through the initial phases. To find real overlaps in curricular concepts requires in-depth dialogue and conversation.

When Is This Shared Model Useful?

The shared curricula model is appropriate when subject matters are clustered into broad bands such as the humanities or practical arts. Also, this model facilitates early stages of implementation toward integrated curricula. It is a viable model to use with two disciplines as an intermediary step to teams of four disciplines that are much more complicated and complex. However, it is a model that truly looks for those "roots running underground" because they bring cohesiveness to the curricula. This is the model that really searches for the conceptual understandings that are designated to be enduring—learning that follows students into real-world experiences.

Figures 5.2, 5.3, and 5.4 are examples of completed shared models of integration, and Figure 5.5 provides the opportunity for readers to record their own design for this model.

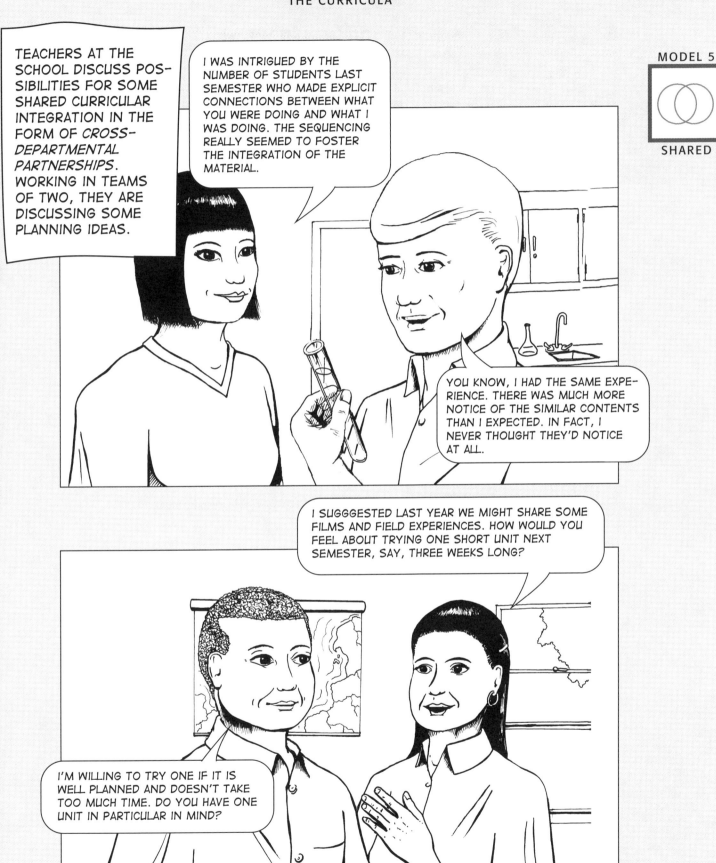

MODEL 5

SHARED

SAMPLE 1 FOR SHARED MODEL

MODEL 5

SHARED

Choose a partner from another department. Think about particular units of study or topics of concern that each of you teach. Find two units—one unit you teach and one unit your partner teaches—that seem to make a logical or commonsense match. Using the Venn diagram, take turns talking and writing in the outer circles about the units. Go in-depth in the conversation, telling your partner specifically what you do in the unit. Then, find the concepts, skills, or attitudes (the content and the process standards) that the two units share in common. Use the most robust idea to create a thematic focus or a skill focus.

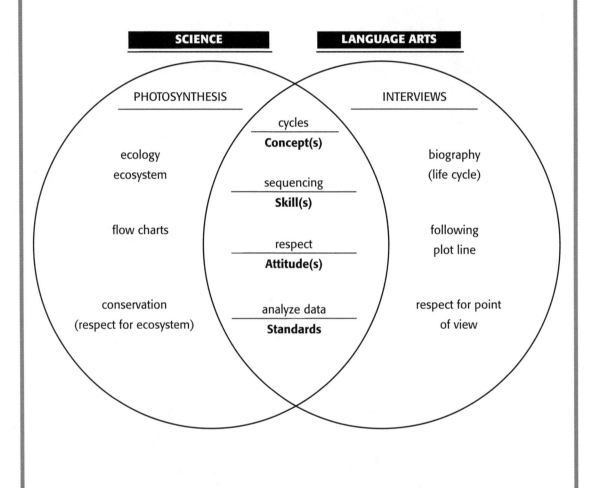

NOTES & REFLECTIONS

Topics and units from two related disciplines offer rich possibilities for integration by identifying basic concepts, skills, attitudes, and standards that overlap.

Figure 5.2

SAMPLE 2 FOR SHARED MODEL

MODEL 5

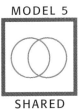

SHARED

Choose a partner from another department. Think about particular units of study or topics of concern that each of you teach. Find two units—one unit you teach and one unit your partner teaches—that seem to make a logical or commonsense match. Using the Venn diagram, take turns talking and writing in the outer circles about the units. Go in-depth in the conversation, telling your partner specifically what you do in the unit. Then, find the concepts, skills, or attitudes (the content and the process standards) that the two units share in common. Use the most robust idea to create a thematic focus or a skill focus.

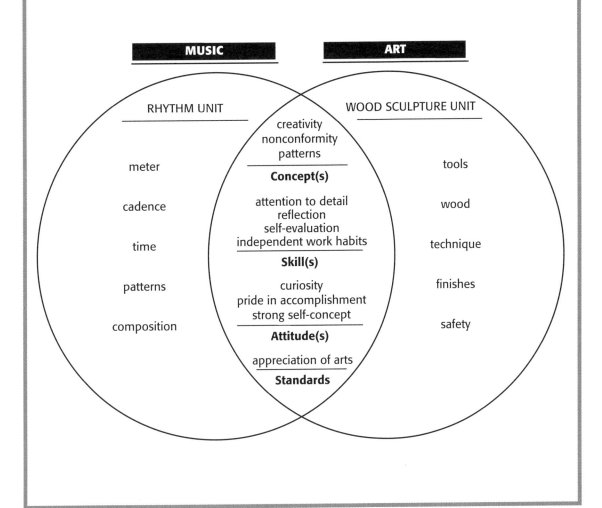

NOTES & REFLECTIONS

Figure 5.3

SAMPLE 3 FOR SHARED MODEL

MODEL 5

SHARED

Choose a partner from another department. Think about particular units of study or topics of concern that each of you teach. Find two units—one unit you teach and one unit your partner teaches—that seem to make a logical or commonsense match. Using the Venn diagram, take turns talking and writing in the outer circles about the units. Go in-depth in the conversation, telling your partner specifically what you do in the unit. Then, find the concepts, skills, or attitudes (the content and the process standards) that the two units share in common. Use the most robust idea to create a thematic focus or a skill focus.

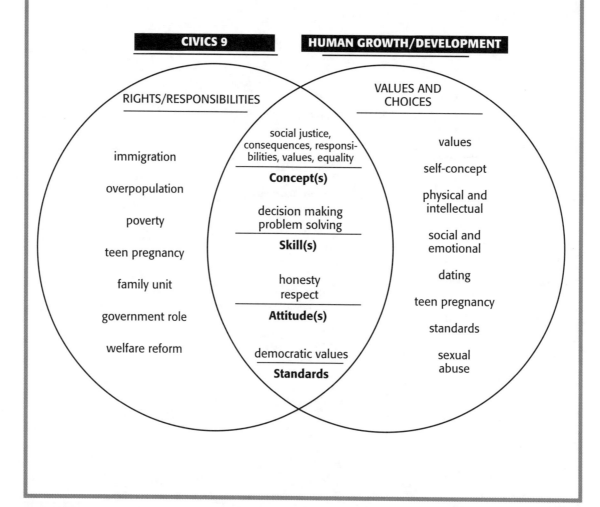

NOTES & REFLECTIONS

Figure 5.4

SkyLight Professional Development

DESIGN FOR SHARED MODEL

MODEL 5

SHARED

Choose a partner from another department. Think about particular units of study or topics of concern that each of you teach. Find two units—one unit you teach and one unit your partner teaches—that seem to make a logical or commonsense match. Using the Venn diagram, take turns talking and writing in the outer circles about the units. Go in-depth in the conversation, telling your partner specifically what you do in the unit. Then, find the concepts, skills, or attitudes (the content and the process standards) that the two units share in common. Use the most robust idea to create a thematic focus or a skill focus.

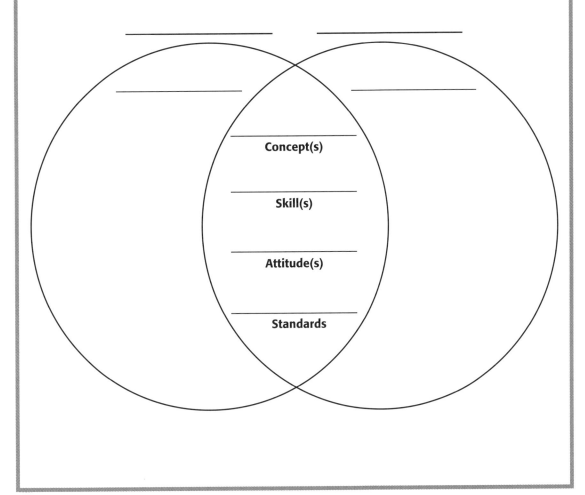

NOTES & REFLECTIONS

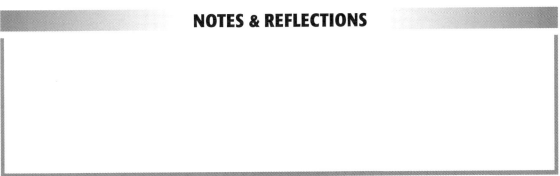

Figure 5.5

SkyLight Professional Development

Webbed

Webbed curricula represent the thematic
approach to integrating subject matter.

W E B B E D

Telescope—broad view of an entire constellation as one theme, webbed to the various elements

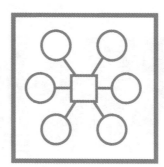

Webbed curricula represent the thematic approach to integrating subject matter.

Example
The teacher presents a simple topical theme, such as the circus, and webs it to the subject areas. A conceptual theme, such as conflict, can be webbed for a broader reach in the theme approach.

"We must open the doors of opportunity. But we must also equip our people to walk through those doors."—Lyndon B. Johnson

What Is the Webbed Model?

Webbed curricula represent the thematic approach to integrating subject matter. Typically, this thematic approach to curriculum development begins with a theme such as transportation or inventions. After a cross-departmental team has made this decision, it uses the theme as an overlay to the different subjects: inventions lead to the study of simple machines in science, reading and writing about inventors in language arts, designing and building models in industrial arts, drawing and studying Rube Goldberg contraptions in mathematics, and making flow charts in computer technology classes. In more sophisticated webbings, intricate units of study can be developed in which integration occurs in all relevant areas to cluster and address standards through robust curriculum models.

What Does It Look Like?

In departmentalized situations, the webbed curricular approach to integration is often achieved through the use of a fairly generic but fertile theme such as patterns or cycles. This conceptual theme provides rich possibilities for the inherent diversities of the various disciplines.

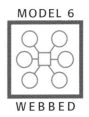

MODEL 6

WEBBED

While similar conceptual themes such as structures or conflict provide fertile ground for cross-disciplinary units of study, the elementary models can also use a book or a genre of books as the topic to thematically organize their curricula. For example, fairy tales or dog stories can become catalysts for curricular webbing. Typical lists look like Figure 6.1.

A Look at Webbed Models

CONCEPTS	TOPICS	PROBLEMS
• freedom	• space	• hostages
• cooperation	• birds	• recycling
• challenge	• Canada	• school funding
• conflict	• reactions	• revolution
• discovery	• the world	• drought/flood
• culture	• WWI	• cultural clash
• change	• rain forest	• pollution
• argument & evidence	• partnerships	• energy crisis
• perseverance	• kites	• war

Figure 6.1

What Does It Sound Like?

When searching for a theme, teacher teams generally begin with an idea-gathering session that sounds like a lot of genuine interaction, conversation, and dialogue among colleagues: "How 'bout this one?" "What do you think of this?" "I read about a school that used cultural diversity as an overriding theme." "Let's brainstorm a long list. I don't want to use the first one we think of just to be done with it." "Maybe we should ask the students for their ideas." "I have some lists of theme ideas from a workshop." "Yeah, but we will need to look at that list carefully and compare them to some criteria. I have Perkin's criteria here." And so it goes as they explore possibilities and set guidelines for reaching a decision. Figure 6.2 provides criteria for selecting possible themes.

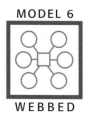

MODEL 6

WEBBED

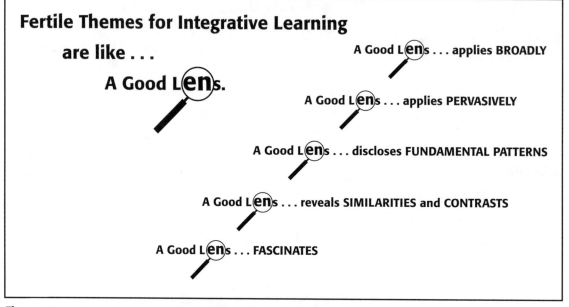

Fertile Themes for Integrative Learning
are like . . .
A Good Lens.

A Good Lens . . . applies BROADLY

A Good Lens . . . applies PERVASIVELY

A Good Lens . . . discloses FUNDAMENTAL PATTERNS

A Good Lens . . . reveals SIMILARITIES and CONTRASTS

A Good Lens . . . FASCINATES

Figure 6.2 From "Selecting Fertile Themes for Integrated Learning," by D. N. Perkins in H. H. Jacobs, ed., 1989, *Interdisciplinary Curriculum: Design and Implementation,* pp. 67–76, Arlington, VA: Association for Supervision and Curriculum Development.

What Are the Advantages?

An advantage of the webbed approach to curricular integration is the motivational factor that results from selecting high-interest themes. In addition, the webbed model or unit-writing approach is familiar to seasoned teachers and is a fairly straightforward curriculum planning model for less experienced teachers to grasp. Thematic units are multidisciplinary units that make it easy to address the various content standards, yet keep an overall focus or pattern. The webbed model also facilitates teamwork planning as cross-departmental teams work to weave a theme into all content areas. The thematic approach or webbed model provides a visible and motivational umbrella for students. It is easy for them to see how different activities and ideas are connected.

What Are the Disadvantages?

The most serious difficulty with the webbed model lies in the selection of a theme. There is a tendency to grab at shallow themes that are superficially useful in curriculum planning. Often these artificial themes lead to a contrived curriculum. Also, caution must be used not to sacrifice the logical and necessary scope and sequence inherent in the disciplines. In this model, teachers can get bogged down in curriculum writing that may not warrant the time involved as compared to long-term use of the thematic unit in years to come. Yet, if a theme is used from year to year, so that, over time, a number of thematic units have been developed and "banked" for re-use, the time is worth it. Another disadvantage is that teachers can become focused on activities rather than on concept development in this model, so caution should be used to keep the content relevant and rigorous.

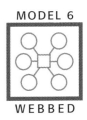

MODEL 6

WEBBED

When Is This Webbed Model Useful?

The webbed model for integrating curriculum is a team approach that takes time to develop. Summer curriculum writing time is an opportune period to initiate this model so teachers can fully explore theme options and set criteria for quality. This model often takes planning and coordination among the various departments and special subject areas. It is a great model to use when trying a two- to four-week interdisciplinary pilot unit. Because of the planning needed to do this model well, it is advisable to start with a manageable piece of the curriculum.

Instead of webbing a theme to the various disciplines, try using multiple intelligences for each cell in the grid (Gardner 1983, 1999). Figure 6.3 shows the eight intelligences—verbal/linguistic, visual/spatial, logical/mathematical, musical/rhythmic, interpersonal/social, intrapersonal/introspective, bodily/kinesthetic, and naturalist. Develop a grid with eight columns and try to place activities for the different intelligences for each cell in the grid.

Figures 6.4, 6.5, and 6.6 are examples of completed webbed model integration exercises, and Figure 6.7 provides the opportunity for readers to record their own design for this model. Figure 6.8 shows a grid with the eight intelligences and ideas for types of activities. Figure 6.9 is a grid for the teachers to use to identify specific readings or activities for each intelligence as an integrated unit is developed around the multiple intelligences. It is just a variation of the webbed model that targets differentiated learning through the multiple intelligences.

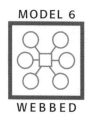

MODEL 6

WEBBED

MULTIPLE WAYS TO EXPERIENCE LEARNING

Verbal/ Linguistic	Visual/ Spatial	Logical/ Mathematical	Musical/ Rhythmic	Interpersonal/ Social	Intrapersonal/ Introspective	Bodily/ Kinesthetic	Naturalist
reporting	storyboarding	reasoning	singing	discussing	journaling	dancing	observing
writing essays	painting	collecting	listening	responding	feeling	sculpting	discovering
creating stories	cartooning	recording	playing	dialoging	reflecting	performing	uncovering
reciting	observing	analyzing	composing	interviewing	logging	preparing	observing
listing	drawing	graphing	audiotaping	surveying	meditating	constructing	digging
telling/ retelling	illustrating	comparing/ contrasting	improvising	questioning	studying	acting	planting
listening	diagramming	classifying	recording	paraphrasing	rehearsing	role playing	comparing
labeling	depicting	ranking	selecting music	clarifying	self-assessing	dramatizing	displaying
dialoging	showing	evaluating	critiquing music	affirming	remembering	pantomiming	sorting

Figure 6.3

SkyLight Professional Development

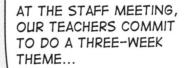

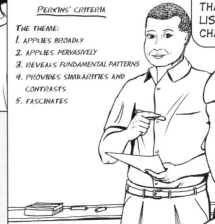

SAMPLE 1 FOR WEBBED MODEL

MODEL 6

WEBBED

Using a list of themes, select one for the team that seems to meet the criteria for fertile themes. Add a kid-friendly tagline to the theme to give it more focus (e.g., Fashion: Whose Statement Is It?). Then, work around the web, labeling the various disciplines and slotting learning experiences for each. Complete the discussion by adding spokes to each subject area to indicate the targeted standards and assessments.

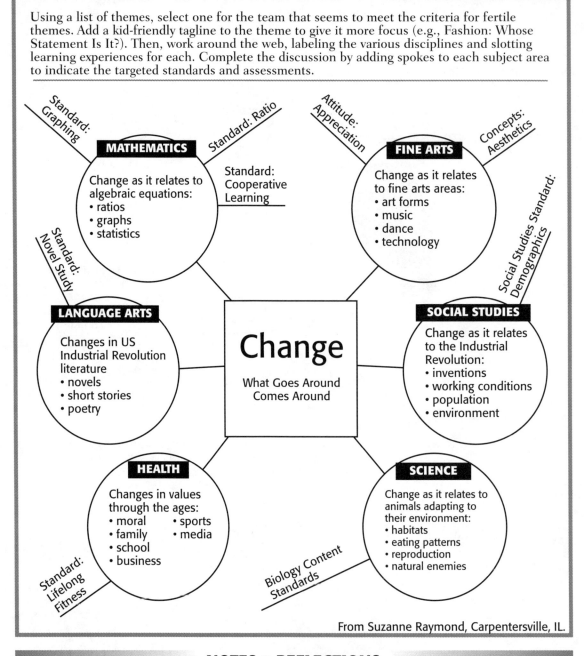

From Suzanne Raymond, Carpentersville, IL.

NOTES & REFLECTIONS

In this webbed model, the theme provides a fresh lens with which to frame and view content. The theme acts as a common umbrella that is visible to students as they work in the various content areas. It also provides a way to look at the various standards (see spokes on circles) that are addressed in a robust, thematic unit. It is an easy integration model for the learner.

Figure 6.4

SAMPLE 2 FOR WEBBED MODEL

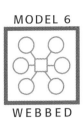
Using a list of themes, select one for the team that seems to meet the criteria for fertile themes. Add a kid-friendly tagline to the theme to give it more focus (e.g., Fashion: Whose Statement Is It?). Then, work around the web, labeling the various disciplines and slotting learning experiences for each. Complete the discussion by adding spokes to each subject area to indicate the targeted standards and assessments.

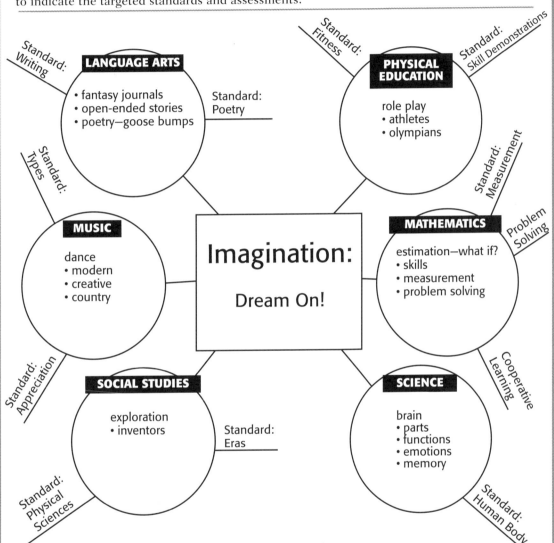

NOTES & REFLECTIONS

Figure 6.5

MODEL 6

WEBBED

SAMPLE 3 FOR WEBBED MODEL

Using a list of themes, select one for the team that seems to meet the criteria for fertile themes. Add a kid-friendly tagline to the theme to give it more focus (e.g., Fashion: Whose Statement Is It?). Then, work around the web, labeling the various disciplines and slotting learning experiences for each. Complete the discussion by adding spokes to each subject area to indicate the targeted standards and assessments.

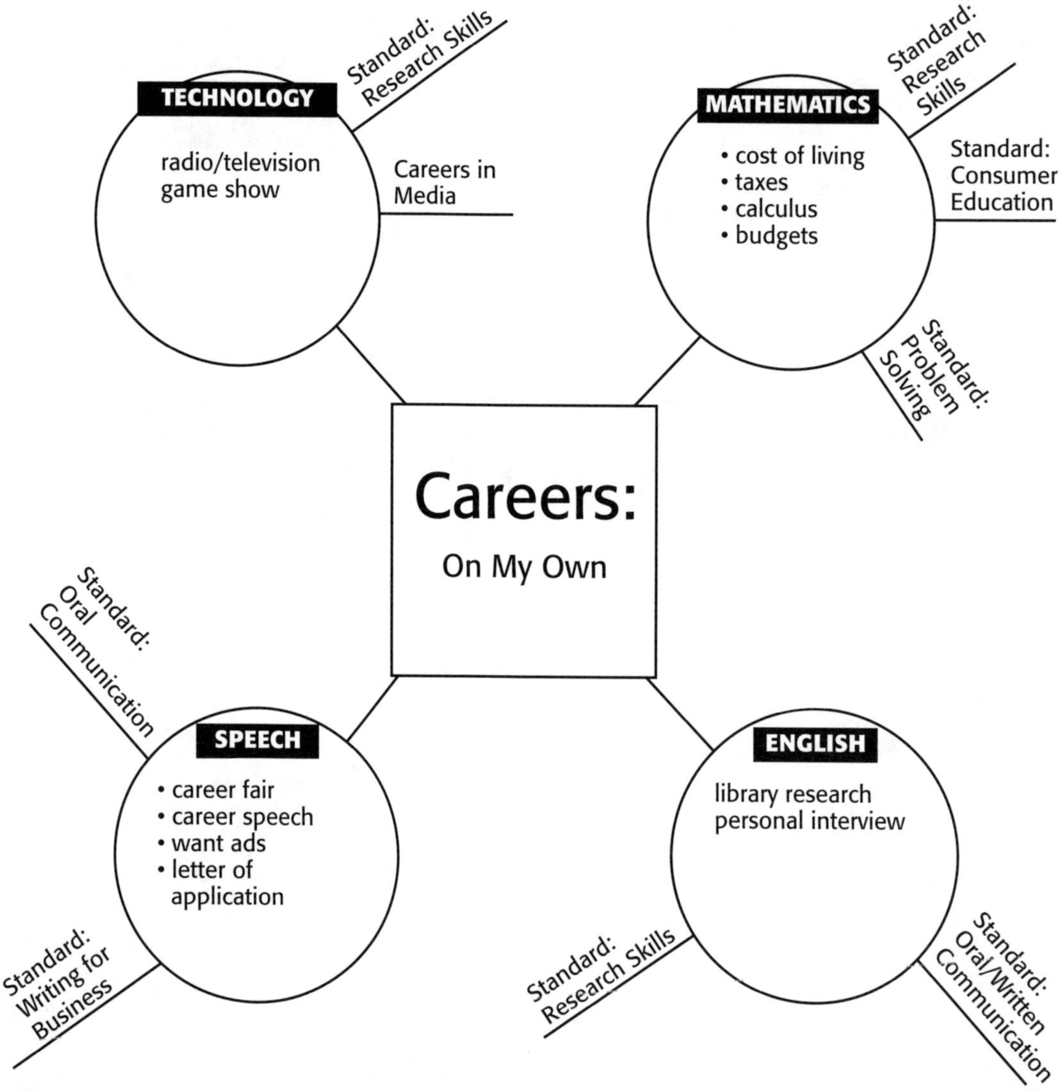

Standard: Research Skills

TECHNOLOGY

radio/television game show

Careers in Media

Standard: Research Skills

MATHEMATICS

• cost of living
• taxes
• calculus
• budgets

Standard: Consumer Education

Standard: Problem Solving

Careers:
On My Own

Standard: Oral Communication

SPEECH

• career fair
• career speech
• want ads
• letter of application

Standard: Writing for Business

ENGLISH

library research
personal interview

Standard: Research Skills

Standard: Oral/Written Communication

NOTES & REFLECTIONS

Figure 6.6

DESIGN FOR WEBBED MODEL

MODEL 6

WEBBED

Using a list of themes, select one for the team that seems to meet the criteria for fertile themes. Add a kid-friendly tagline to the theme to give it more focus (e.g., Fashion: Whose Statement Is It?). Then, work around the web, labeling the various disciplines and slotting learning experiences for each. Complete the discussion by adding spokes to each subject area to indicate the targeted standards and assessments.

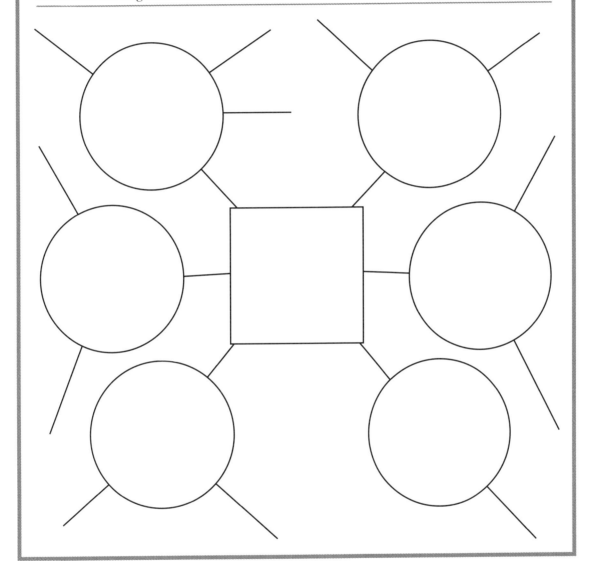

NOTES & REFLECTIONS

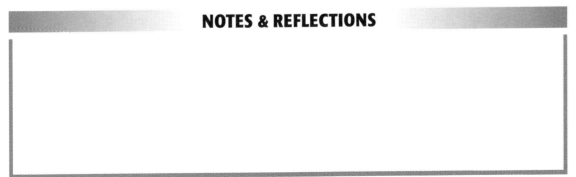

Figure 6.7

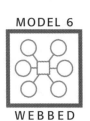

MODEL 6

WEBBED

MULTIPLE TYPES OF ACTIVITIES

Verbal/Linguistic	Visual/Spatial	Logical/Mathematical	Musical/Rhythmic	Interpersonal/Social	Intrapersonal/Introspective	Bodily/Kinesthetic	Naturalist
Printouts	Mosaics	Mazes	Performance	Group Projects	Journals	Role Playing	Field Trips (Farm/Zoo)
Debates	Paintings	Puzzles	Songs	Group Tasks	Meditations	Dramatizing	Field Studies
Poetry	Drawings	Outlines	Musicals	Observation	Self-Assessments	Skits	Bird Watching
Jokes	Sketches	Matrices	Instruments	Charts	Intuiting	Body Language	Observing
Speeches	Illustrations	Sequences	Rhythms	Social Interactions	Logs	Facial Expressions	Nests
Reading	Cartoons	Patterns	Compositions	Dialogs	Records	Experiments	Planting
Storytelling	Sculptures	Logic	Harmonies	Conversations	Reflections	Dancing	Photographing
Listening	Models	Analogies	Chords	Debates	Quotations	Gestures	Nature Walks
Audiotapes	Constructions	Timelines	Trios/Duos	Arguments	"I" Statements	Pantomiming	Forecasting Weather
Essays	Maps	Equations	Quartets	Consensus	Creative Expression	Field Trips	Star Gazing
Reports	Storyboards	Formulas	Beat	Communication	Goals	Lab Work	Fishing
Crosswords	Videotapes	Theorems	Melodies	Collages	Affirmations	Interviews	Exploring Caves
Fiction	Photographs	Calculations	Raps	Murals	Insight	Sports	Categorizing Rocks
Nonfiction	Symbols	Computations	Jingles	Mosaics	Poetry	Games	Ecology Studies
Newspapers	Visual Aids	Syllogisms	Choral	Round Robins	Interpretations	Manipulatives	Catching Butterflies
Magazines	Posters	Codes	Readings	Sports	Writing	Investigations	Shell Collecting
Internet Research	Murals	Games	Scores	Games	Sketching	Walk Abouts	Identifying Plants
Books	Doodles	Probabilities	Choirs	Challenges	Doodling	Explorations	
Biographies	Statues	Fractions	Chorus	Teamwork	Wondering	Hands-On Learning	
Bibliographies	Collages	Problem Solving	Listening		Musing	Simulations	
Internet Research	Mobiles	Measurement	Recording				
Web	Graphics	Metric					
	Comics						
	Ads						

Figure 6.8

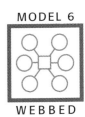

MODEL 6

WEBBED

UNIT:

List specific activities for each intelligence in its column to relate to the overall topic or concept targeted in the theme.

Verbal/ Linguistic	Visual/ Spatial	Logical/ Mathematical	Musical/ Rhythmic	Interpersonal/ Social	Intrapersonal/ Introspective	Bodily/ Kinesthetic	Naturalist

Figure 6.9

Threaded

Standards, thinking skills, social skills, study skills, graphic organizers, technology, and a multiple intelligences approach to learning thread through all disciplines.

THREADED

Magnifying glass—life skills that magnify all content through a metacurricular approach

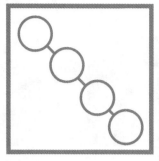

Standards, thinking skills, social skills, study skills, graphic organizers, technology, and a multiple intelligences approach to learning thread through all disciplines.

Example
The teaching staff targets prediction in reading, mathematics, and science lab experiments while the social studies teacher targets predicting current events, and thus threads prediction across all four disciplines.

"The great end of an education is to discipline rather than to furnish the mind. To train it to the use of its own powers rather than to fill it with the accumulation of others."
—*Tryon Edwards*

What Is the Threaded Model?

Standards, thinking skills, social skills, study skills, graphic organizers, technology, and a multiple intelligences approach to learning thread through all disciplines. This threaded model of curricular integration focuses on the metacurriculum that supersedes or intersects the very heart of any and all subject matter content. For example, prediction is a skill used to estimate in mathematics, forecast in current events, anticipate in a novel, and hypothesize in the science lab. Consensus-seeking strategies are used in resolving conflicts in any problem-solving situation. These skills are, in essence, threaded through standard curricular content. They are "life skills" that can be targeted with various content successfully.

What Does It Look Like?

It looks like writing across the content or reading across the disciplines. Using the idea of a meta-curriculum, grade-level or interdepartmental teams target a set of thinking skills to infuse into the existing content priorities. For example, using the thinking skills chart in Figure 7.1, "compare and contrast" might be the thinking skill the freshmen team chooses to thread across content. Likewise, a multiple intelligence (picked from Figure 7.2), a social skill (drawn from Figure 7.3), a study skill, a standard (see Figure 7.4), a graphic organizer, or a performance could be threaded through the various disciplines.

MODEL 7

THREADED

Examples of Thinking Skills as Threads

Balancing your choices with skills from critical thinking clusters and creative thinking clusters, select microskills to thread through the curriculum for a period of time. By changing the skill each month or so, various thinking habits are reinforced for the students as the skills are threaded into the classwork throughout the school. Students encounter the skills in different contexts.

CRITICAL THINKING SKILLS

Attribute Cluster of Skills
  Classify
  Compare and contrast
  Sequence
  Prioritize
  Solve analogies

Analysis Cluster of Skills
  Analyze for bias
  Analyze for assumptions
  Draw conclusions

Evaluation Cluster of Skills
  Evaluate
  Solve analogies
  Analyze assumptions
  Analyze bias
  Critique

Sequence Cluster of Skills
  Sequence
  Prioritize
  Discern cause and effect
  Draw conclusions

MACROPROCESSES
  Problem Solving
  Decision Making
  Creative Ideation

GRAPHIC ORGANIZERS
  Web
  Map
  Flowchart
  Venn
  Matrix
  Fishbone
  KWL
  PMI
  Thought tree
  Chain of events

CREATIVE THINKING SKILLS

Perception Cluster of Skills
  Predict
  Image
  Invent
  Hypothesize
  Visualize
  Discern patterns

Inference Cluster of Skills
  Predict
  Infer
  Imply
  Generalize
  Hypothesize

Brainstorm Cluster Skills
  Personify
  Brainstorm
  Invent
  Visualize
  Associate
  Discern patterns

Figure 7.1

Examples of Multiple Intelligences as Threads

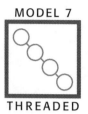

MODEL 7

THREADED

Using Gardner's theory of multiple intelligences, select from the eight identified intelligences and thread one through the content for a period of time. (Some schools thread a different intelligence each month as a way to familiarize teachers, students, and parents with the theory of multiple intelligences.) Looking at prodigies in a field helps illustrate the various dimensions of each intelligence.

Verbal/Linguistic Intelligence: Abilities in reading, writing, speaking, and listening
Prodigies: Writing—Maya Angelou
              Speaking—Martin Luther King
              Reading—Abraham Lincoln
              Listening—Johnny Carson

Visual/Spatial Intelligence: Abilities in the visual arts, architecture, and design
Prodigies: Painting—Claude Monet
              Sculpture—Auguste Rodin
              Architecture—Frank Lloyd Wright
              Design—Jackson Pollock

Mathematical/Logical Intelligence: Abilities in mathematical ideas, logic, and reasoning
Prodigies: Mathematics—Sir Issac Newton
              Logic—Albert Einstein
              Reasoning—Aristotle

Musical/Rhythmic Intelligence: Ability to appreciate, compose, and perform musically
Prodigies: Appreciation—Leonard Bernstein
              Composing—Wolfgang Amadeus Mozart
              Performing—Itzak Perlman

Interpersonal/Social Intelligence: Abilities with interpersonal relationships in the social realm
Prodigies: Interpersonal skills—John F. Kennedy
              Relationships—Dale Carnegie
              Social realm—Florence Nightingale

Intrapersonal/Introspective Intelligence: Abilities to understand the inner world of the self, to understand intrinsic motivations, and to know oneself
Prodigies: Inner world—Mahatma Gandhi
              Intrinsic motivation—Bertrand Russell
              Know thyself—Socrates

Bodily/Kinesthetic Intelligence: Abilities to develop body, awareness to manipulate the muscles, and develop motor agility
Prodigies: Develop body awareness—Michael Jordan
              Manipulate the muscles—Margot Fonteyn
              Motor agility—Tiger Woods

Naturalist/Physical World Intelligence: Abilities to understand, relate to, and classify the natural world.
Prodigies: Animal species—Charles Darwin
              Classify birds—James Audebon
              Sea—Jacques Cousteau
              Planetary universe—Carl Sagan

Figure 7.2

Examples of Social Skills as Threads

MODEL 7

THREADED

Select appropriate social skills to thread through the various classes. Choose from the four major categories of social skills: communication, team building/trust, leadership, and conflict resolution. By varying the category, students are exposed to a number of social skills over time.

Communication Skills	Team Building/ Trust	Leadership	Conflict Resolution
• Use 6" voice • Listen to others • Clarify • Paraphrase • Give examples • Sense tone • Associate ideas • Extend ideas • Affirm others	• Keep an open mind • Respect each other's opinion • Accept others' ideas • Listen with focus • Build on each other's ideas	• Help each other • Take responsibility • Accept a group role • Contribute ideas • Let all participate • Encourage others • Include all members • Synthesize ideas	• Disagree with the idea, not the person • Seek consensus • Generate alternatives • Reach consensus • Justify ideas • Learn how to "agree to disagree"

Figure 7.3

Generic Standards of Learning as Threads

Students will acquire knowledge and skills to:
- Identify problems and their elements.
- Speak and write standard English.
- Justify sound decisions.
- Understand democratic principles.
- Perform and produce works of art.
- Compute numerical functions.
- Organize data into useful forms.
- Use the principles of movement.
- Discover and evaluate patterns.

Figure 7.4

What Does It Sound Like?

As the standards, thinking skills, social skills, graphic organizers, or multiple intelligences are threaded into the content, the teacher asks appropriate questions such as: "How did you think about that?" "What thinking skill did you find most helpful?" "How well did your group work today?" and "Have you used your musical intelligences today?" These processing questions contrast sharply with the

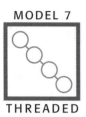

MODEL 7

THREADED

usual cognitive questions such as "What answer did you get?" and "How many agree?" (Sometimes, the metacognitive questions sound to the kids like the teacher is off the track. Students will often say, "OK, what are we supposed to do?" to try to get to the task at hand).

What Are the Advantages?

Advantages of the threaded model revolve around the concept of the metacurriculum. This metacurriculum is the awareness and control of the skills and strategies of thinking and learning that go beyond the subject matter content. Teachers stress the metacognitive behavior so students learn about *how* they are learning. By making students aware of the learning processes, future transfer is facilitated. The plus is that, in this integration model, not only does the content stay pure for each discipline, but also the students reap the added benefit of an extraordinary kind of thinking that can transfer into life skills.

What Are the Disadvantages?

A disadvantage of the threaded model is the necessity of adding "another" curriculum, such as a thinking or social skills curriculum. Content connections across subject matter are not addressed explicitly. The metacurriculum surfaces, but the disciplines remain static. Connections between and among the content matter of the subjects are not necessarily stressed. Also, in order to thread the metacurriculum through the content, all teachers need an understanding of those skills and strategies.

When Is This Threaded Model Useful?

The threaded model is used to integrate curricula when a metacurriculum of thinking and social skills is a district focus. This model is appropriate to use as one of the alternative steps toward a more intense subject matter integration. The threaded model is easier to sell to hard core curriculum advocates who are reluctant to shift the subject matter priorities. Therefore, this becomes a viable senior high model to start with as teachers keep their content intact and infuse thinking, cooperating, and multiple intelligences into that content. Figures 7.5, 7.6, and 7.7 are examples of completed threaded model integration exercises, and Figure 7.8 provides the opportunity for readers to record their own design for this model.

OUR TEACHERS FIND IT EASY TO THREAD CERTAIN SKILLS SUCH AS INFERRING THROUGH THEIR PARTICULAR CONTENTS . . .

SO, OUR TEACHER TEAMS WILL FOCUS ON THE THINKING SKILL OF INFERENCING. THE SCIENCE CLASSES WILL TARGET INFERENCE AND OBSERVATION AS KEY SKILLS.

RIGHT, BOB. INFERRING FROM DATA AND PREDICTING TRENDS, BOTH IN A HISTORICAL SENSE AND IN FUTURE STUDIES, ALSO HAS POTENTIAL TO ENRICH THE CURRICULUM CONTENT. AT FIRST, I WAS AFRAID THE SUBJECT MATTER WOULD LOSE AND WE WOULD DILUTE THE DISCIPLINES, BUT THIS ACTUALLY IS ENHANCING MY CONTENT!

MARIA, INFERRING FROM GRAPHS, CHARTS, AND DATA IS A NATURAL FOR MATH CLASS. WITH THE OVERLOAD OF INFORMATION AND THE INCREASED USE OF GRAPHICS, STUDENTS NEED WORK IN MAKING INFERENCES FROM THE GATHERED DATA. IT'S A RICH THREAD TO STRING THROUGH CONTENTS.

READING BETWEEN THE LINES—MAKING INFERENCES IS AN ABSOLUTE BASIC EXPECTATION OF GOOD READERS. I THINK THE STUDY OF LITERATURE THIS SEMESTER WILL BE EXPECTED TO GO BEYOND THE LITERAL INFORMATION PRESENTED.

MODEL 7

THREADED

SKILL SAMPLE FOR THREADED MODEL

Working as a cross-disciplinary team, think about the skills teachers expect students to develop and use across content areas. Compile a list of some of the most common skills encountered in the various disciplines (predicting, reaching agreement, persuasion, organization, problem solving, making decisions) and select one skill to focus on for an agreed-upon period of time and to thread into the different subject matters. Meet periodically to discuss the impact of the threading in the different classes. Also, try threading several threads at once.

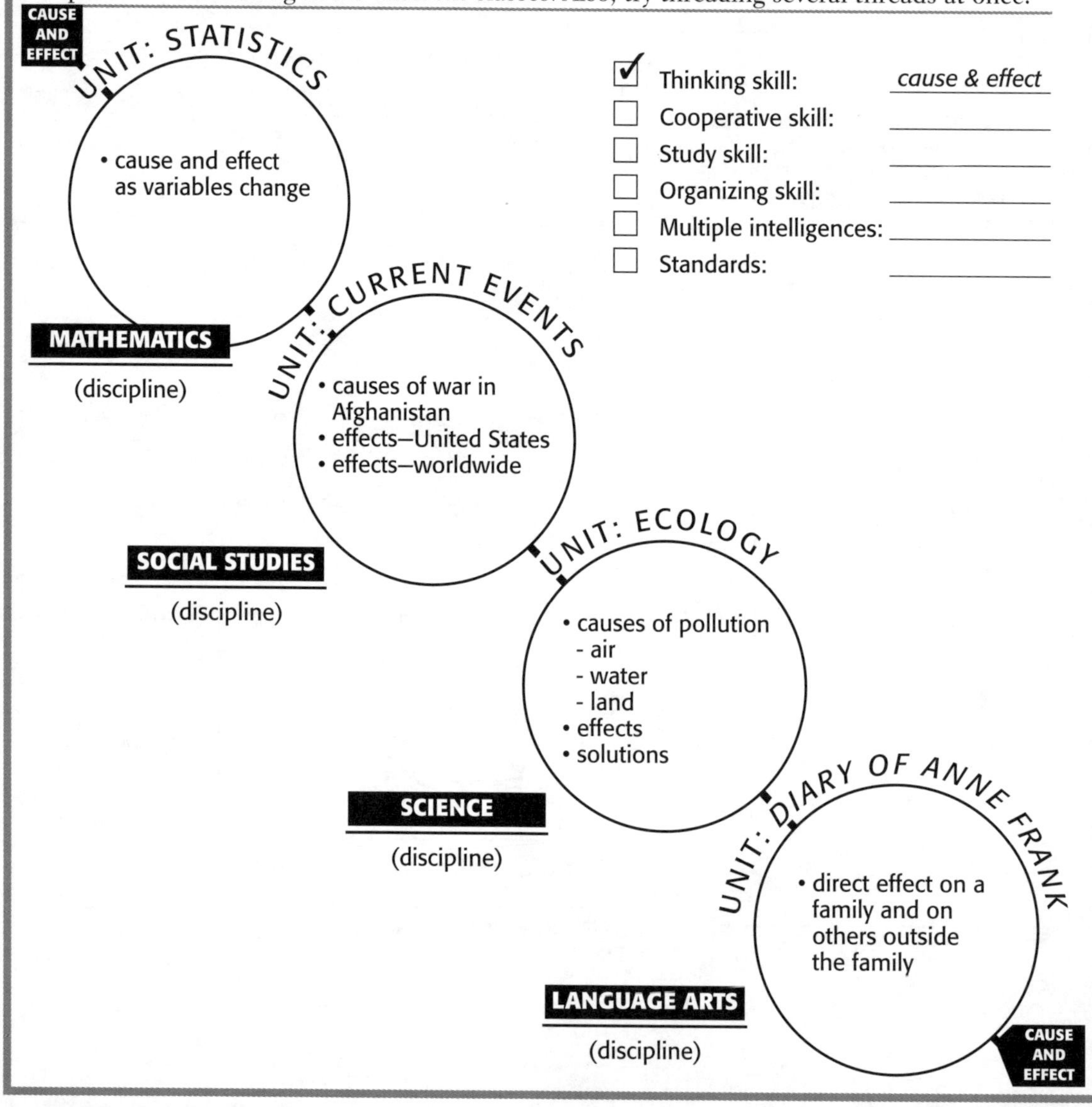

CAUSE AND EFFECT

UNIT: STATISTICS

• cause and effect as variables change

MATHEMATICS

(discipline)

UNIT: CURRENT EVENTS

• causes of war in Afghanistan
• effects—United States
• effects—worldwide

SOCIAL STUDIES

(discipline)

- ☑ Thinking skill: _cause & effect_
- ☐ Cooperative skill: _____
- ☐ Study skill: _____
- ☐ Organizing skill: _____
- ☐ Multiple intelligences: _____
- ☐ Standards: _____

UNIT: ECOLOGY

• causes of pollution
 - air
 - water
 - land
• effects
• solutions

SCIENCE

(discipline)

UNIT: DIARY OF ANNE FRANK

• direct effect on a family and on others outside the family

LANGUAGE ARTS

(discipline)

CAUSE AND EFFECT

NOTES & REFLECTIONS

Threading the thinking skill (or metacurriculum) through the subject matter content takes some consensus from the team members. However, there is no watering down of content in the respective disciplines. It is an amiable teaching model with positive outcomes for students.

Figure 7.5

MULTIPLE INTELLIGENCES SAMPLE FOR THREADED MODEL

MODEL 7

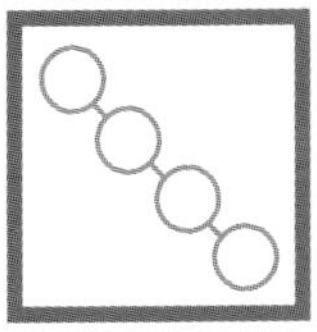

THREADED

Working as a cross-disciplinary team, think about the skills teachers expect students to develop and use across content areas. Compile a list of some of the most common skills encountered in the various disciplines (predicting, reaching agreement, persuasion, organization, problem solving, making decisions) and select one skill to focus on for an agreed-upon period of time and to thread into the different subject matters. Meet periodically to discuss the impact of the threading in the different classes. Also, try threading several threads at once.

BODILY/ KINES- THETIC

UNIT: CULTURAL MASKS

Create a mask.

ART
(discipline)

UNIT: ANCIENT GREECE

Act out a Greek myth.

SOCIAL STUDIES
(discipline)

UNIT: PARTS OF SPEECH

Act out parts of speech.

LANGUAGE ARTS
(discipline)

UNIT: STUDY OF ELEMENTS

Form the components of an atom.

SCIENCE
(discipline)

BODILY/ KINES- THETIC

☐ Thinking skill: _____
☐ Cooperative skill: _____
☐ Study skill: _____
☐ Organizing skill: _____
☑ Multiple intelligences: *bodily/kinesthetic*
☐ Standards: _____

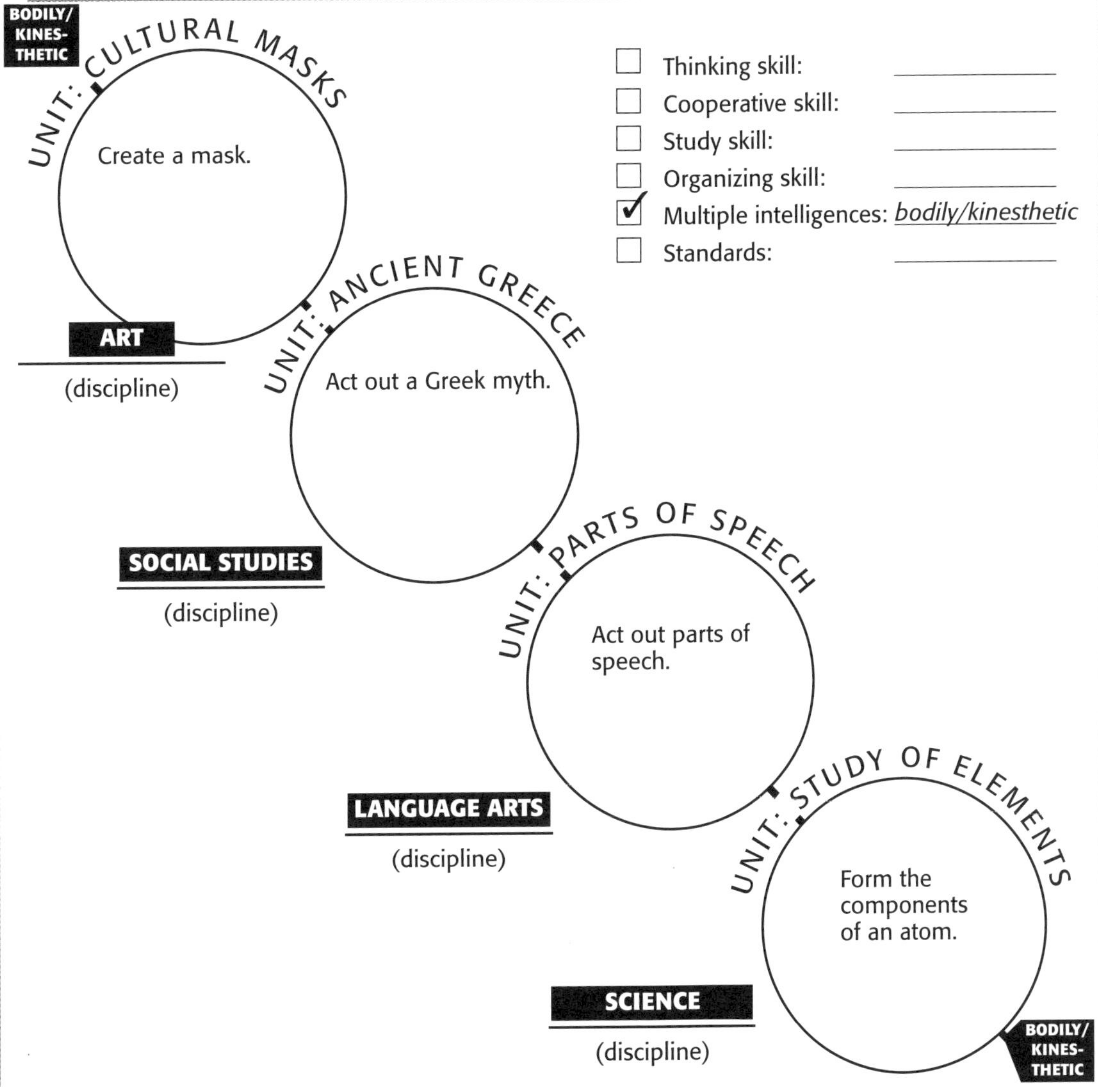

NOTES & REFLECTIONS

Figure 7.6

STANDARDS SAMPLE FOR THREADED MODEL

MODEL 7

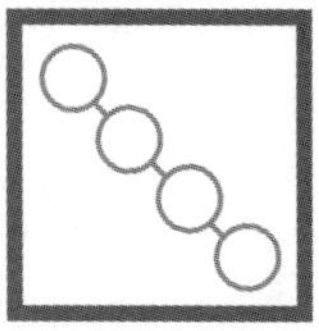

THREADED

Working as a cross-disciplinary team, think about the skills teachers expect students to develop and use across content areas. Compile a list of some of the most common skills encountered in the various disciplines (predicting, reaching agreement, persuasion, organization, problem solving, making decisions) and select one skill to focus on for an agreed-upon period of time and to thread into the different subject matters. Meet periodically to discuss the impact of the threading in the different classes. Also, try threading several threads at once.

PROBLEM SOLVING

UNIT: PRINT MEDIA

Resolve source credibility.

MEDIA

(discipline)

☐ Thinking skill: _____
☐ Cooperative skill: _____
☐ Study skill: _____
☐ Organizing skill: _____
☐ Multiple intelligences: _____
☑ Standards: *problem solving*

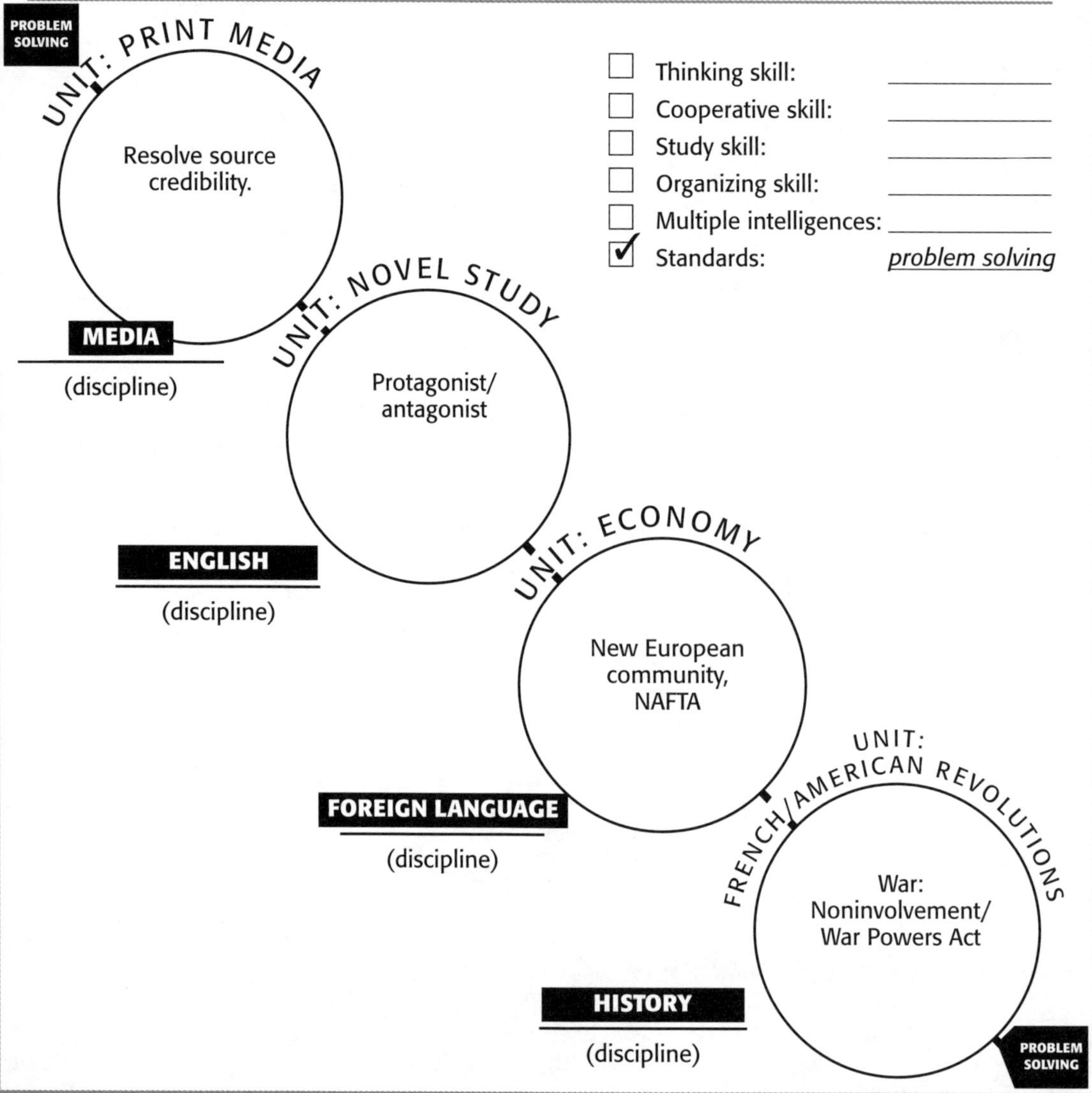

UNIT: NOVEL STUDY

Protagonist/ antagonist

ENGLISH

(discipline)

UNIT: ECONOMY

New European community, NAFTA

FOREIGN LANGUAGE

(discipline)

UNIT: FRENCH/AMERICAN REVOLUTIONS

War: Noninvolvement/ War Powers Act

HISTORY

(discipline)

PROBLEM SOLVING

NOTES & REFLECTIONS

Figure 7.7

DESIGN FOR THREADED MODEL

MODEL 7

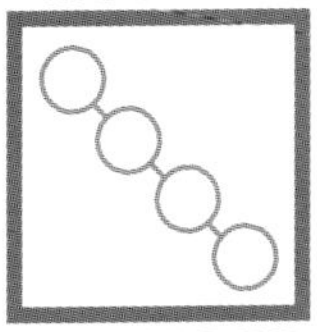

THREADED

Working as a cross-disciplinary team, think about the skills teachers expect students to develop and use across content areas. Compile a list of some of the most common skills encountered in the various disciplines (predicting, reaching agreement, persuasion, organization, problem solving, making decisions) and select one skill to focus on for an agreed-upon period of time and to thread into the different subject matters. Meet periodically to discuss the impact of the threading in the different classes. Also, try threading several threads at once.

☐ Thinking skill: _____

☐ Cooperative skill: _____

☐ Study skill: _____

☐ Organizing skill: _____

☐ Multiple intelligences: _____

☐ Standards: _____

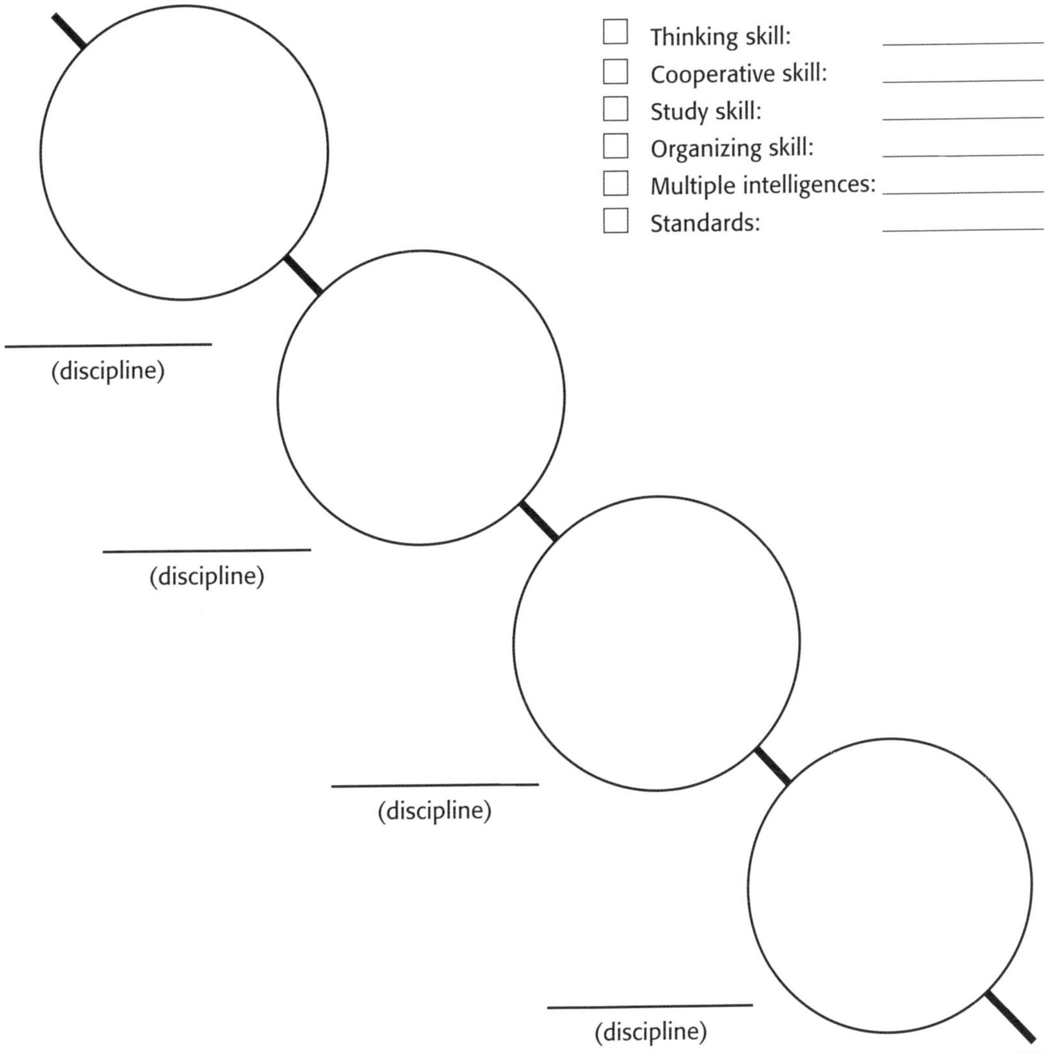

_____
(discipline)

_____
(discipline)

_____
(discipline)

_____
(discipline)

NOTES & REFLECTIONS

Figure 7.8

Integrated

The integrated curricular model represents a cross-disciplinary approach similar to the shared model.

INTEGRATED

Kaleidoscope—new patterns and designs that use the basic elements of each discipline

The integrated curricular model represents a cross-disciplinary approach similar to the shared model.

Example

In mathematics, science, social studies, fine arts, language arts, and practical arts, teachers look for patterns and approach content through these patterns in all the discipline areas.

"I call a complete and generous education that which fits [an individual] to perform justly, skillfully, and magnanimously all the offices, both private and public, of peace and war."—John Milton

What Is the Integrated Model?

The integrated curricular model represents a cross-disciplinary approach similar to the shared model. The integrated model blends the four core disciplines by setting curricular priorities in each and finding the overlapping skills, concepts, and attitudes in all four. As in the shared model, the integration is a result of sifting ideas out of subject matter content, not laying an idea over the subjects as in the webbed themes approach. The integration sprouts from within the various disciplines, and matches are made among them as commonalities emerge. This is an inductive approach to curriculum integration, rather than a deductive approach as in the webbed model. In fact, this model really is the ultimate integration model because the patterns and themes truly do emerge from the various subject matter units. In essence, teachers continue to teach their content, but their focus takes on a bigger meaning that stretches to other content.

What Does It Look Like?

In the middle school or secondary school, an integrated curriculum is conceived as an interdisciplinary team struggles with an overloaded curriculum. As a team, they decide to "selectively abandon" pieces from the traditional curriculum. Armed with content standards for the discipline, the four team members begin to explore overlapping priorities and concepts that undergird their disciplines. One such overlap they discover early on is the concept of "argument and evidence." It works well in mathematics, science, language arts, and social studies. It is a first step.

In the elementary classroom, an integrated model that illustrates the critical elements of this approach is the literacy movement in which reading, writing, listening, and speaking skills spring from a literature-based program that taps all the energies of the learner and the disciplines. Literacy is learning that embraces an integrated curriculum as opposed to the more traditional, fragmented model in which each subject is addressed separately and apart from the others. Integrated models such as literacy are designed with the learner as the focus, while fragmented models are designed with the content as the focal point.

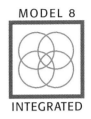

MODEL 8

INTEGRATED

What Does It Sound Like?

M. C. Richards (1980) says, "Unless we educate for wholeness in person and wholeness of our earth planet, we are not really intelligent. In our school subjects, we have an opportunity to study humankind as a family, and the heart as the body of that family. We have the possibility of developing a curriculum which is like a map of its dreams and its history, a map of interconnections. Interdisciplinary methods try to avoid squeezing the life out of one part and blowing it up in another."

What Are the Advantages?

A distinct advantage of the integrated model is the ease with which the learner is lead to the interconnectedness and interrelationships among the various disciplines. The integrated model builds understanding across departments and fosters appreciation of staff knowledge and expertise. The integrated model, when successfully implemented, approaches the ideal learning environment for an integrated day externally and for an integrated learner focus internally. The

MODEL 8

INTEGRATED

integrated model also carries with it an inherent motivational factor as students and ideas gain momentum from class to class. The authentic projects and performances that result from this kind of deep integration are perfect platforms to integrate mathematics, science, social studies, and language arts with the visual, performing, and practical arts.

What Are the Disadvantages?

It is a difficult, sophisticated model to implement fully. This integrated model requires highly skilled staff who are confident in the content standards, skills, and attitudes that pervade their respective disciplines. In addition, the integrated curriculum requires interdepartmental teams with blocks of planning and teaching time in common, which often means major restructuring of schedules. To integrate curricula with explicit attention to the genuine conceptual priorities of each discipline requires the commitment of a myriad of resources.

When Is This Integrated Model Useful?

This integrated model is most appropriately used with a cross-departmental team of volunteers who are willing to commit time and energy to the integration process. It is helpful to start with a small pilot project such as a three- to four-week unit. Summer curriculum-writing time or designed release time during the semester is most likely necessary to fully explore this model.

After a pilot is in place, further team commitment can be made. But, a word of caution is needed here. It is not advisable for a school to adopt this model as a schoolwide reform without first giving it serious thought. Remember, committed volunteers across departments are the critical elements for this complex model. Eventually, as team members work together learning about the other disciplines and the other team members, the units can be planned for longer periods of time. But this is a gradual process of building confidence and trust as team curriculum designers. However, after a team commits to the integrated model, the projects and performances that result become unforgettable learning experiences for students.

Figures 8.1, 8.2, and 8.3 are examples of completed integrated model integration exercises, and Figure 8.4 provides the opportunity for readers to record their own design for this model.

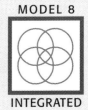

MODEL 8

INTEGRATED

MEANWHILE, OVER THE SUMMER, MEETINGS AT THE SCHOOL ARE FREQUENT AND HEATED. OUR TEACHERS AND THE PRINCIPAL, PRISCILLA, ARE EXPLORING POSSIBILITIES AND LOOKING FOR MATCH-UPS.

I LIKED THE WEBBED MODEL WE TRIED LAST YEAR. BUT I SOMETIMES FELT LIKE I WAS MANIPULATING AND CONTRIVING MY CONTENT A BIT. WHAT IF WE TRIED A FULL-BLOWN INTERDISCIPLINARY TEAM APPROACH THIS YEAR AND LOOKED FOR THE NATURAL OVERLAPS?

I AGREE, SUE. BUT WHAT IF WE ONLY FIND A FEW GENUINE AREAS OF OVERLAP? HOW DO WE COME TO TERMS WITH THAT WITHOUT ARTIFICIALLY STRETCHING OUR TRUE PRIORITIES? LET'S TRY THE INTEGRATED APPROACH IN A PILOT ONLY. MAYBE PLAN A THREE-WEEK SEGMENT . . .

I THINK I KNOW WHAT YOU MEAN, TOM. WE SHOULD FIRST LOOK AT OUR INDIVIDUAL CONTENT PRIORITIES AND THEN SIFT OUT CONCEPTS, IDEAS, AND ATTITUDES THAT HAVE OVERLAPPING ELEMENTS. FOR EXAMPLE, MY DNA UNIT. ASIDE FROM THE TECHNICAL INFORMATION ABOUT GENETIC ENGINEERING, THERE ARE MORAL AND ETHICAL ISSUES THAT OVERLAP WITH SOCIAL STUDIES AND LANGUAGE ARTS. THERE ARE ALSO A NUMBER OF MATHEMATICAL CONCEPTS INHERENT TO THE DNA MODEL.

THAT'S AN EXCITING IDEA! I LIKE COMING FROM THE HEART OF EACH DISCIPLINE AND THEN LOOKING FOR THE OVERLAPPING CONCEPTS. LET'S GO FOR IT!

HOW TO

INTEGRATE
THE CURRICULA

SAMPLE 1 FOR INTEGRATED MODEL

MODEL 8

INTEGRATED

As an interdisciplinary or grade level team, take turns and talk and write about the units or topics in each of the different disciplines that occur at one time. Tell in some detail what occurs during units. As the discussion progresses, use an inductive approach, and see what bubbles up in the center; look for overlaps and commonalities among the various subjects. Find the big ideas that could serve as themes for all the subjects represented in the integrated unit and proceed to develop essential questions from each discipline to drive the theme.

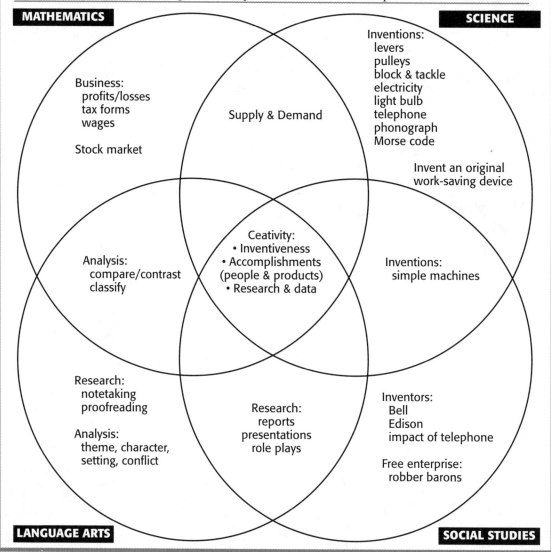

From Kathleen Vehring, Carpentersville, IL.

NOTES & REFLECTIONS

Using their content priorities, team members look beyond the topics to the concepts, skills, and attitudes they target in their separate disciplines. Armed with these basics, the team looks for the overlapping ideas that emerge as common ground among the four disciplines. The similarities emerge from the content pieces.

Figure 8.1

SkyLight Professional Development

SAMPLE 2 FOR INTEGRATED MODEL

MODEL 8

INTEGRATED

As an interdisciplinary or grade level team, take turns and talk and write about the units or topics in each of the different disciplines that occur at one time. Tell in some detail what occurs during units. As the discussion progresses, use an inductive approach, and see what bubbles up in the center; look for overlaps and commonalities among the various subjects. Find the big ideas that could serve as themes for all the subjects represented in the integrated unit and proceed to develop essential questions from each discipline to drive the theme.

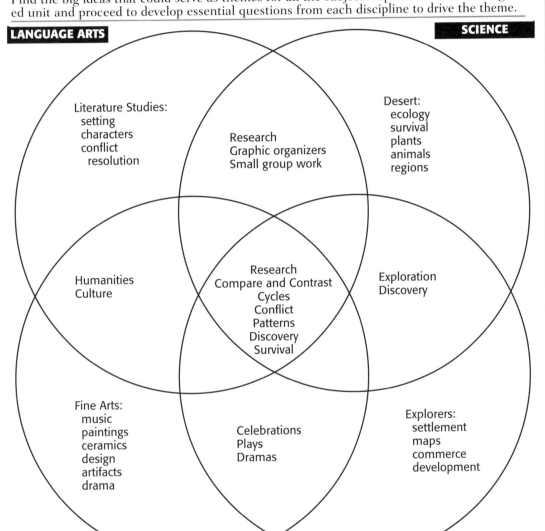

LANGUAGE ARTS

Literature Studies:
setting
characters
conflict
resolution

Research
Graphic organizers
Small group work

SCIENCE

Desert:
ecology
survival
plants
animals
regions

Humanities
Culture

Research
Compare and Contrast
Cycles
Conflict
Patterns
Discovery
Survival

Exploration
Discovery

Fine Arts:
music
paintings
ceramics
design
artifacts
drama

Celebrations
Plays
Dramas

Explorers:
settlement
maps
commerce
development

ARTS

SOCIAL STUDIES

NOTES & REFLECTIONS

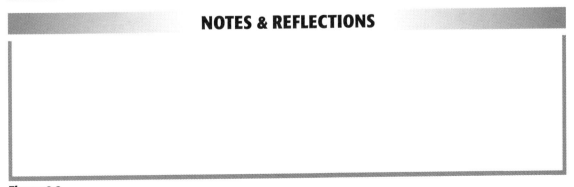

Figure 8.2

SAMPLE 3 FOR INTEGRATED MODEL

MODEL 8

INTEGRATED

As an interdisciplinary or grade level team, take turns and talk and write about the units or topics in each of the different disciplines that occur at one time. Tell in some detail what occurs during units. As the discussion progresses, use an inductive approach, and see what bubbles up in the center; look for overlaps and commonalities among the various subjects. Find the big ideas that could serve as themes for all the subjects represented in the integrated unit and proceed to develop essential questions from each discipline to drive the theme.

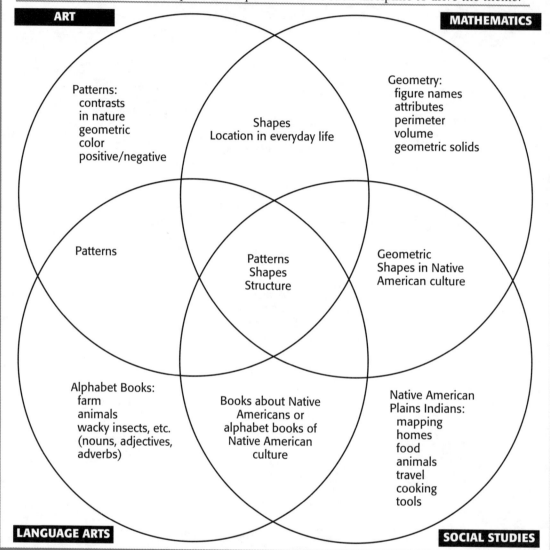

ART

Patterns:
contrasts
in nature
geometric
color
positive/negative

Shapes
Location in everyday life

MATHEMATICS

Geometry:
figure names
attributes
perimeter
volume
geometric solids

Patterns

Patterns
Shapes
Structure

Geometric
Shapes in Native
American culture

Alphabet Books:
farm
animals
wacky insects, etc.
(nouns, adjectives,
adverbs)

Books about Native
Americans or
alphabet books of
Native American
culture

Native American
Plains Indians:
mapping
homes
food
animals
travel
cooking
tools

LANGUAGE ARTS

SOCIAL STUDIES

NOTES & REFLECTIONS

Figure 8.3

SkyLight Professional Development

DESIGN FOR INTEGRATED MODEL

As an interdisciplinary or grade level team, take turns and talk and write about the units or topics in each of the different disciplines that occur at one time. Tell in some detail what occurs during units. As the discussion progresses, use an inductive approach, and see what bubbles up in the center; look for overlaps and commonalities among the various subjects. Find the big ideas that could serve as themes for all the subjects represented in the integrated unit and proceed to develop essential questions from each discipline to drive the theme.

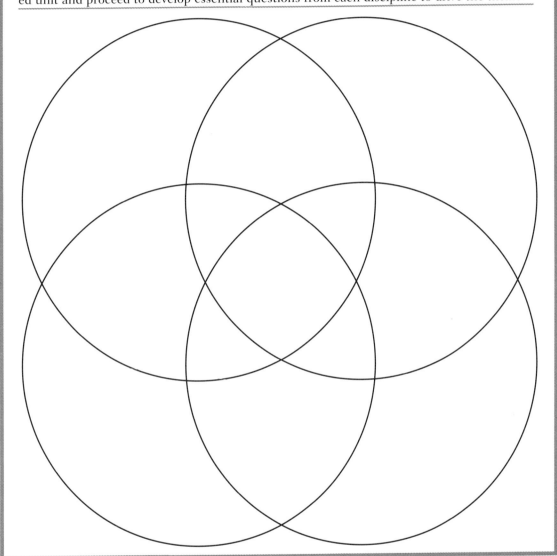

NOTES & REFLECTIONS

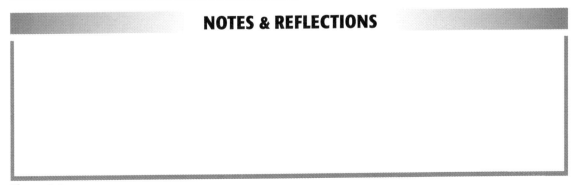

Figure 8.4

Immersed

The individual integrates all data, from every
field and discipline, by funneling the ideas through
his or her area of interest.

I M M E R S E D

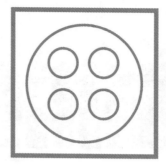

The individual integrates all data, from every field and discipline, by funneling the ideas through his or her area of intense interest.

Microscope—intensely personal view that allows microscopic exploration as all content is filtered through lens of interest and expertise

Example
A student or doctoral candidate has an area of expert interest and sees all learning through that lens.

"The one real object of education is to have a [person] in the condition of continually asking questions."
—Bishop Mondell Creighton

What Is the Immersed Model?

Aficionados, art students, mentees, graduate students, doctoral candidates, and post-doctoral fellows are totally immersed in a field of study. They filter all curricular content learning through one microscopic lens. The individual integrates all data, from every field and discipline, by funneling the ideas through his or her area of intense interest. In this model of integrated curricula, the integration is internally and intrinsically accomplished by the learner with little or no extrinsic or outside intervention. It is real-world integration.

What Does It Look Like?

At the university level, a doctoral candidate is immersed in biochemistry. Her area of specialization is chemical bonding of substances. Even though her field is chemistry, she devours the software programs in computer science classes so she can analyze her data in simulated lab experiments, saving days of tedious lab work. She accepts

an offer to learn patent law in order to protect her ideas for her company and to protect her company from liability cases. All learning paths are sparked by her passion for her field.

Likewise, a first grader writes incessantly about butterflies, bugs, spiders, insects, and creepy crawlies of all sorts. Her artwork is modeled on the symmetrical design of ladybugs and the patterns of butterflies. She counts and mounts, frames and sings about them. Her interest in insect biology is already consuming her. The books she chooses reflect her internal integration of her interest in learning her subject.

What Does It Sound Like?

An immersed learner might say something like this: "I'm totally immersed in my work. It is a labor of love and my laboratory is my life. It seems that everything I choose to pursue with any fervor is directly related to my intellectual interest." Just as the writer records notes or the artist makes sketches, the immersed learner is constantly making connections to his subject. With this self-directed, self-initiating learner, the teacher's mission often becomes one of getting out of the learner's way.

What Are the Advantages?

Of course, the ultimate advantage is that integration must take place within the learner, which is exactly what is illustrated in this model. The learner is self-driven by an insatiable hunger to understand. "The more we know, the more we know we don't know" becomes an unhidden truth. As the student digs deeper into a field of interest, the related areas and new pathways seem unending. Actually, the immersed learner exhibits phenomenal discipline as he or she develops this intense focus. Of course, another plus is that the connection making of this learner is often made explicit to other learners as the expert makes advances in the field.

ALL LEARNING—MATHEMATICS, SCIENCE, HISTORY, LANGUAGE ARTS—IS FILTERED THROUGH THE LEARNER'S LENS OF EXPERIENCE AND EXPERTISE.

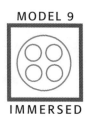

MODEL 9

IMMERSED

What Are the Disadvantages?

The filtering of all ideas through a single microscopic lens may occur too prematurely or in too narrow a focus. Richness of experience and broad bases from which to review a specialization bring depth and dimension to the learner's perspective. A liberal background that cuts across the major disciplines provides the most fertile ground for enriching this learner's experience—the more varied, in fact, the better, at least early in the educational process. There is plenty of time to specialize later.

When Is This Immersed Model Useful?

As teachers strive to differentiate curricula, they use the immersed model as part of the various units of study. They direct students to choose an area of interest within a given framework and to pursue that area as a special project within the unit. When students select an area, they often become more invested in it and begin to integrate disciplines as they work on the project.

In other situations, such as career academies, high school students are already being asked to find their areas of strengths and choose a preliminary path of study that is connected to the careers in those stronger academic areas. Some select the arts academy, while others prefer the health and sciences academy or the business academy. These learners practice the immersed model as they learn things through the lens of their career interest.

Immersion often begins as a hobby or a labor of love that directs the learning of the student because of an intense interest in the area. Eventually, a student filters all learning through the lens of this interest, making natural connections across many disciplines.

Figures 9.1, 9.2, and 9.3 are examples of completed immersion model integration exercises, and Figure 9.4 provides an opportunity for readers to record their own design for this model.

A GRADUATE OF THE INTEGRATED CURRICULUM SCHOOL, AND THE UNIVERSITY, TELLS HIS COLLEAGUE . . .

I'D BEEN WITH THE FIRM FOR FIVE YEARS AS A CHEMICAL RESEARCHER AND LIKED TO JUST STICK TO THE LABORATORY. BUT THEN I HAD TO LEARN THE CAD/CAM PROGRAMS TO USE THE TECHNICAL EQUIPMENT. THE TIME I SAVED BY USING THE COMPUTER SIMULATIONS WAS UNBELIEVABLE. THEN I STARTED SPENDING A LOT MORE TIME ON THE PATENTING PROCESS AND STARTED LOOKING AT PATENT LAW. NOW THE COMPANY WANTS ME TO GO TO LAW SCHOOL.

NOT ONLY THAT, IN ORDER TO DEAL WITH OUR JAPANESE MANUFACTURERS, I'VE STARTED STUDYING JAPANESE! I NEED SOME UNDERSTANDING OF THE LANGUAGE AND CULTURE. THE LEARNING NEVER STOPS. WHO KNOWS WHAT I'LL GET INTO NEXT!

SAMPLE 1 FOR IMMERSED MODEL

MODEL 9

IMMERSED

To think about how the standard curriculum is integrated through the immersed model, select one student to work with. Through dialogue and discussion, plot his or her learning exposure to the various subjects through his or her lens of intense interest. Use the samples as guides, but let the ideas flow to see how much integration actually occurs through the natural inquiry that is part of intrinsically motivated endeavors.

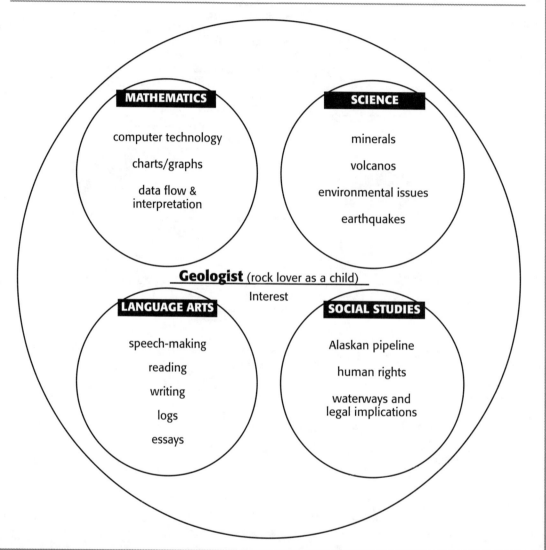

NOTES & REFLECTIONS

The immersed learner funnels most learning through his or her area of interest. This learner uses a refined selection process that automatically screens input and seeks out the areas that have explicit and/or implicit connections. The more expert the expert is, the more fine-tuned the selection process is.

Figure 9.1

SAMPLE 2 FOR IMMERSED MODEL

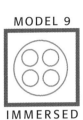
To think about how the standard curriculum is integrated through the immersed model, select one student to work with. Through dialogue and discussion, plot his or her learning exposure to the various subjects through his or her lens of intense interest. Use the samples as guides, but let the ideas flow to see how much integration actually occurs through the natural inquiry that is part of intrinsically motivated endeavors.

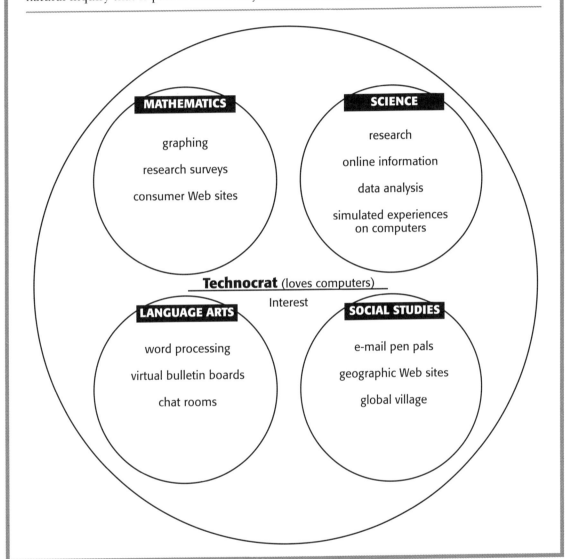

MATHEMATICS

graphing

research surveys

consumer Web sites

SCIENCE

research

online information

data analysis

simulated experiences
on computers

Technocrat (loves computers)

Interest

LANGUAGE ARTS

word processing

virtual bulletin boards

chat rooms

SOCIAL STUDIES

e-mail pen pals

geographic Web sites

global village

NOTES & REFLECTIONS

Figure 9.2

HOW TO INTEGRATE THE CURRICULA

SAMPLE 3 FOR IMMERSED MODEL

MODEL 9

IMMERSED

To think about how the standard curriculum is integrated through the immersed model, select one student to work with. Through dialogue and discussion, plot his or her learning exposure to the various subjects through his or her lens of intense interest. Use the samples as guides, but let the ideas flow to see how much integration actually occurs through the natural inquiry that is part of intrinsically motivated endeavors.

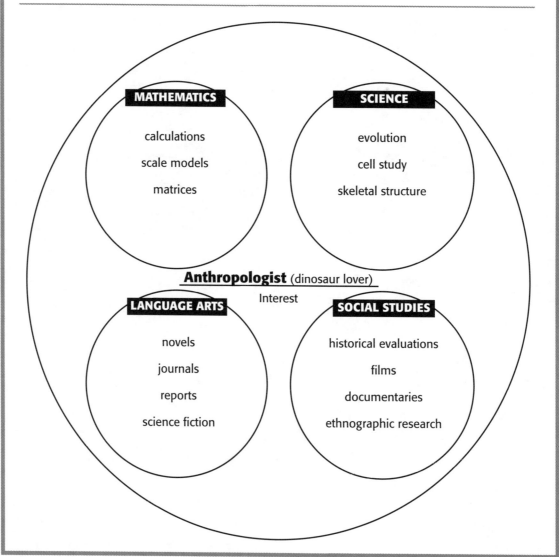

NOTES & REFLECTIONS

Figure 9.3

SkyLight Professional Development

DESIGN FOR IMMERSED MODEL

MODEL 9

IMMERSED

To think about how the standard curriculum is integrated through the immersed model, select one student to work with. Through dialogue and discussion, plot his or her learning exposure to the various subjects through his or her lens of intense interest. Use the samples as guides, but let the ideas flow to see how much integration actually occurs through the natural inquiry that is part of intrinsically motivated endeavors.

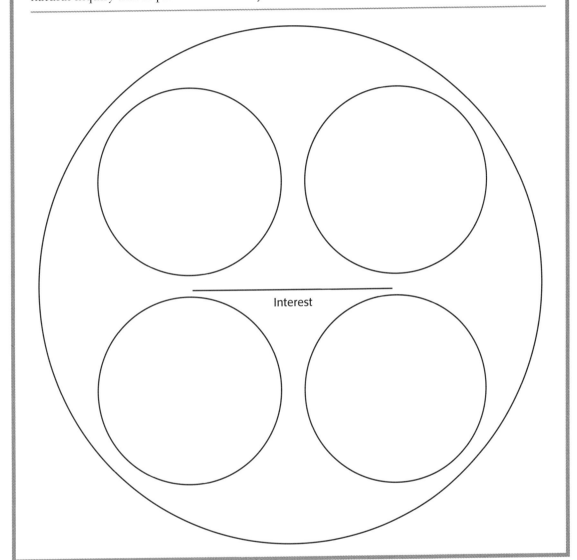

Interest

NOTES & REFLECTIONS

Figure 9.4

Networked

The networked model of integrated learning is an ongoing external source of input, forever providing new, extended, and extrapolated or refined ideas.

N E T W O R K E D

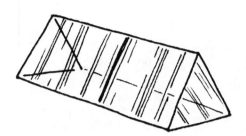

Prism—a view that creates multiple dimensions and directions of focus

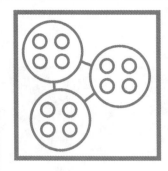

The networked model of integrated learning is an ongoing external source of input, forever providing new, extended, and extrapolated or refined ideas.

Example
An architect, while adapting the CAD/CAM technology for design, networks with technical programmers and expands his or her knowledge base, just as he or she had traditionally done with interior designers.

"The education of a man is never completed until he dies."—Robert E. Lee

What Is the Networked Model?

The networked model of integrated learning is an ongoing external source of input, forever providing new, extended, and extrapolated or refined ideas. The learner's professional network usually grows in obvious, and sometimes not so obvious, directions. In the search for knowledge, learners come to depend on this network as a primary source of information that they must filter through their own lens of expertise and interest.

In the networked model of integration, unlike in the earlier models, the learner directs the integration process through self-selection of the needed networks. Only the learners themselves, knowing the intricacies and dimensions of their field, can target the necessary resources. This model, like the others, develops and grows over time as needs propel the learner in new directions.

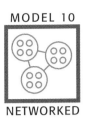

MODEL 10

NETWORKED

What Does It Look Like?

This model of networked integration is seen to a limited extent in the elementary school. Imagine a fifth grader who has maintained a keen interest in Native Americans since his toddler days of playing cowboys and Indians. His passion for Native American lore leads him into historical readings—both fictional and nonfictional. His family, well aware of his intrigue with the Native Americans, hears about an archeological dig that recruits youngsters to actually participate in the dig as part of a summer program offered by a local college. As a result of this summer camp, this learner meets people in a number of fields: an anthropologist, a geologist, an archeologist, an illustrator, and a student of the fine arts, who was hired to represent the dig in drawings. This learner's networks are already taking shape. His natural interest has led him to others in the field who offer various levels of knowledge and insight that extend his learning.

What Does It Sound Like?

The networked model sounds like a three- or four-way conference call that provides various avenues of exploration and explanation. Although these diverse ideas may not come all at once, the networked learner is open to multiple modes of input as divergent components are sifted and sorted to suit the need. This model sounds like the network news—pulling in pictures and stories from around the globe. The network is much like a satellite beaming signals here and there and receiving signals from everywhere.

What Are the Advantages?

The advantages of the networked model are many. This integrated learning approach is extremely proactive in nature, with the learner self-initiating the searches and following the newly emerging paths. The learner is stimulated with relevant information, skill, or concepts that move his or her learning along. The pluses of this model however, cannot be imposed on the learner, but rather must emerge from within. However, mentors can and do provide the necessary models to support this sophisticated stage of learning.

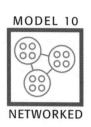

MODEL 10

NETWORKED

What Are the Disadvantages?

The minuses of the networked model are familiar to those who have developed many diverse interests in their labors of love. It is easy to get sidetracked into one of the side ideas. It is also possible to get in over one's head. A particular path may seem inviting and useful, but may suddenly become overwhelming; the benefits no longer outweigh the price one has to pay. Another drawback is that the networked model, if taken to extremes, can spread interests too thin and dilute a concentrated effort.

When Is This Networked Model Useful?

This model, like the immersed model, often moves the onus of integration to the learner rather than to an outside instructional designer. However, it is an appropriate model to present to motivated learners. Tutors or mentors often suggest networking to extend the learner's horizons or provide a needed perspective.

As networks evolve, serendipitous connections appear along the way. Often, these accidental findings propel the learner into new depths in the field or actually lead to the creation of a more specialized field. One such example is the field of genetics, which has developed an area known as genetic engineering. This unfolding of a field is really the result of immersed expert learners networking with other immersed expert learners.

A more explicit example of the networked model is also used in larger high schools. As schools move to the small schools concept and create career academies, students are often expected to network with businesses in their chosen fields. This networking often leads to apprenticeships and/or internships within the career areas of interest. Of course, networking across various disciplines occurs as a natural part of this process.

Figures 10.1, 10.2, and 10.3 are examples of completed network model integration exercises, and Figure 10.4 provides the opportunity for readers to record their own designs for this model. In addition, as a final check for the integration of curricular units, Figure 10.5 is a rubric for integrated curriculum units, Figure 10.6 is a sample of this rubric for an integrated unit on war, and Figure 10.7 is a sample for a theme, *Bridging the Way*.

YEARS LATER . . . A GRADUATE OF THE INTEGRATED SCHOOL IS ON A CONFERENCE CALL WITH TWO NETWORK EXPERTS, A COGNITIVE PSYCHOLOGIST AND A COMPUTER PROGRAMMER.

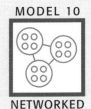

MODEL 10

NETWORKED

LUCY LIBRARIAN

I THINK OF MYSELF AS A LIBRARIAN—THAT WAS MY TRAINING—LIBRARY SCIENCES. BUT AS A DOCTORAL CANDIDATE IN THE AREA OF ARTIFICIAL INTELLIGENCE, I NEED TO NETWORK WITH OTHERS IN THE HIGHLY TECHNICAL FIELDS. I AM SEARCHING FOR A PROGRAM TO HELP SIMULATE A COGNITIVE SEARCH FOR INFORMATION.

SY KEE

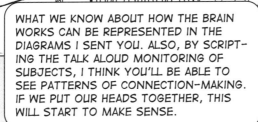

WHAT WE KNOW ABOUT HOW THE BRAIN WORKS CAN BE REPRESENTED IN THE DIAGRAMS I SENT YOU. ALSO, BY SCRIPT-ING THE TALK ALOUD MONITORING OF SUBJECTS, I THINK YOU'LL BE ABLE TO SEE PATTERNS OF CONNECTION-MAKING. IF WE PUT OUR HEADS TOGETHER, THIS WILL START TO MAKE SENSE.

CONNIE COMPUTO

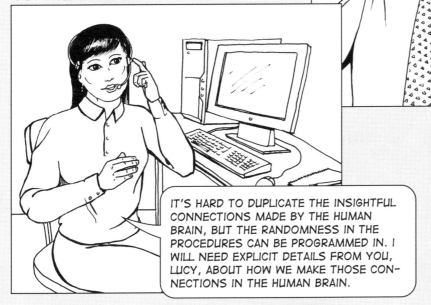

IT'S HARD TO DUPLICATE THE INSIGHTFUL CONNECTIONS MADE BY THE HUMAN BRAIN, BUT THE RANDOMNESS IN THE PROCEDURES CAN BE PROGRAMMED IN. I WILL NEED EXPLICIT DETAILS FROM YOU, LUCY, ABOUT HOW WE MAKE THOSE CON-NECTIONS IN THE HUMAN BRAIN.

NUTRITION AND HEALTH SAMPLE FOR NETWORKED MODEL

MODEL 10

NETWORKED

To work with the networked model, think of a passion, a labor of love, an area of intense interest that one student exhibits. Plot the path of networking opportunities with him or her to record the connected learning experiences that have resulted from or might result from the original seed of interest. Note how an interdisciplinary approach is inherent in this kind of natural pursuit of learning.

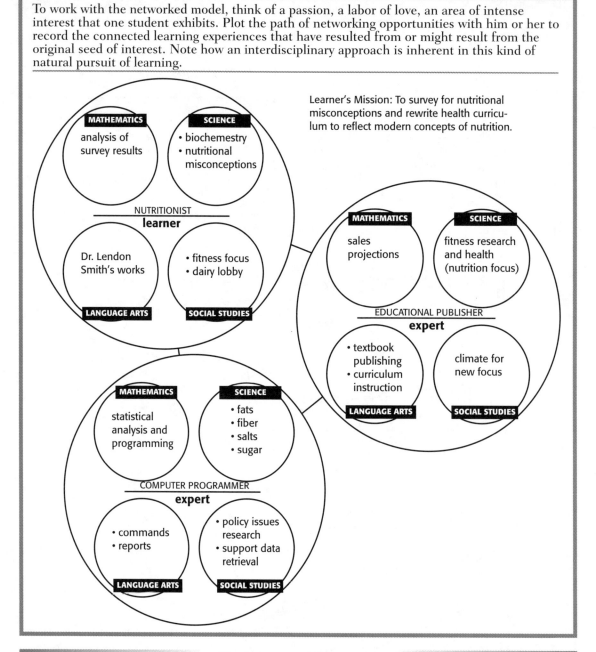

Learner's Mission: To survey for nutritional misconceptions and rewrite health curriculum to reflect modern concepts of nutrition.

Figure 10.1

NOTES & REFLECTIONS

The learner is propelled by his or her area of interest to search out experts both inside and outside the field in order to extend and enrich the field.

POLITICAL INTEREST SAMPLE FOR NETWORKED MODEL

To work with the networked model, think of a passion, a labor of love, an area of intense interest that one student exhibits. Plot the path of networking opportunities with him or her to record the connected learning experiences that have resulted from or might result from the original seed of interest. Note how an interdisciplinary approach is inherent in this kind of natural pursuit of learning.

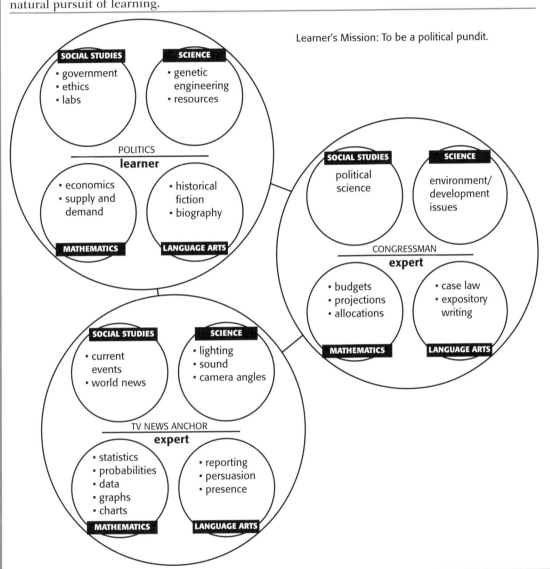

Learner's Mission: To be a political pundit.

POLITICS
learner

SOCIAL STUDIES
• government
• ethics
• labs

SCIENCE
• genetic engineering
• resources

MATHEMATICS
• economics
• supply and demand

LANGUAGE ARTS
• historical fiction
• biography

CONGRESSMAN
expert

SOCIAL STUDIES
political science

SCIENCE
environment/ development issues

MATHEMATICS
• budgets
• projections
• allocations

LANGUAGE ARTS
• case law
• expository writing

TV NEWS ANCHOR
expert

SOCIAL STUDIES
• current events
• world news

SCIENCE
• lighting
• sound
• camera angles

MATHEMATICS
• statistics
• probabilities
• data
• graphs
• charts

LANGUAGE ARTS
• reporting
• persuasion
• presence

NOTES & REFLECTIONS

Figure 10.2

LANGUAGE ARTS SAMPLE FOR NETWORKED MODEL

To work with the networked model, think of a passion, a labor of love, an area of intense interest that one student exhibits. Plot the path of networking opportunities with him or her to record the connected learning experiences that have resulted from or might result from the original seed of interest. Note how an interdisciplinary approach is inherent in this kind of natural pursuit of learning.

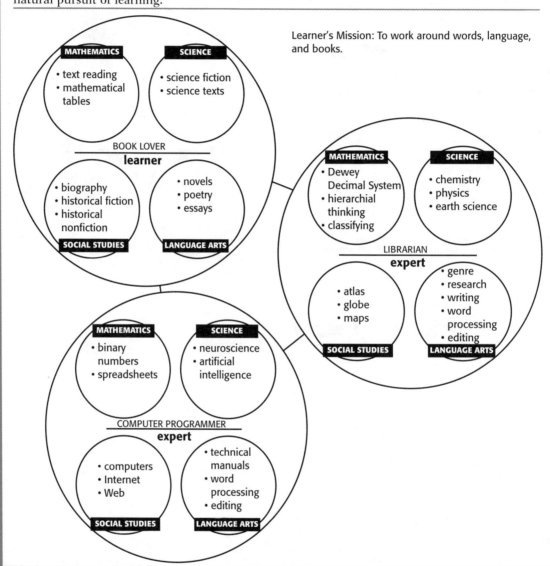

Learner's Mission: To work around words, language, and books.

BOOK LOVER learner

MATHEMATICS
• text reading
• mathematical tables

SCIENCE
• science fiction
• science texts

SOCIAL STUDIES
• biography
• historical fiction
• historical nonfiction

LANGUAGE ARTS
• novels
• poetry
• essays

LIBRARIAN expert

MATHEMATICS
• Dewey Decimal System
• hierarchial thinking
• classifying

SCIENCE
• chemistry
• physics
• earth science

SOCIAL STUDIES
• atlas
• globe
• maps

LANGUAGE ARTS
• genre
• research
• writing
• word processing
• editing

COMPUTER PROGRAMMER expert

MATHEMATICS
• binary numbers
• spreadsheets

SCIENCE
• neuroscience
• artificial intelligence

SOCIAL STUDIES
• computers
• Internet
• Web

LANGUAGE ARTS
• technical manuals
• word processing
• editing

NOTES & REFLECTIONS

Figure 10.3

DESIGN FOR NETWORKED MODEL

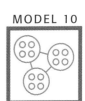
To work with the networked model, think of a passion, a labor of love, an area of intense interest that one student exhibits. Plot the path of networking opportunities with him or her to record the connected learning experiences that have resulted from or might result from the original seed of interest. Note how an interdisciplinary approach is inherent in this kind of natural pursuit of learning.

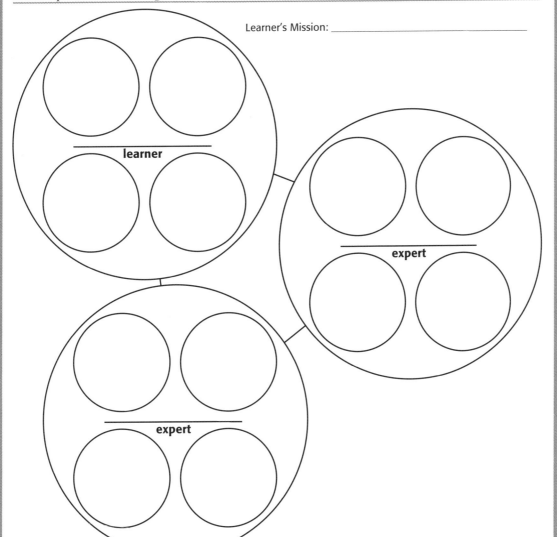

Learner's Mission: _____

learner

expert

expert

NOTES & REFLECTIONS

Figure 10.4

MODEL 10

NETWORKED

MODEL 10

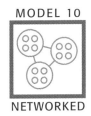

NETWORKED

Rubric for Integrated Curriculum Units of Study

Criteria for Robust Integrated Units	Not Yet!	On Our Way!	This Is It!
RELEVANCE • Meaningful • Purposeful • Life experiences • Real	Inert knowledge	Relates conceptually	Real-world application
RICHNESS Multilayered • Ambiguous • Multiple intelligences • Depth of content	Contrived to fit	Authentic dimensions	Breadth and depth across intelligences
RELATEDNESS • Genuine overlaps • Intentional • Natural hookups across disciplines	No obvious connections across disciplines	Superficial connections across disciplines	Natural, genuine connections across disciplines
RIGOR • Problem solving • Decision making • Higher-order thinking • Expert performance	Pour and store, recall, and regurgitation	Challenge: follow rigorous procedures	Struggle: getting stuck and getting unstuck
RECURSIVENESS • Recurs • Applies • Threads through and carries over • Flops back and returns to	Singular opportunity for concept/skill development	Multiple opportunities for concept/skill development	Transfer of skills and concepts to novel situations through problem solving

Figure 10.5   Extrapolated from Doll, 1973. ASCD/IMSA Consortium for Interdiscipline, Atlanta, 1994.

MODEL 10

NETWORKED

Sample of Integrated Unit: War—How Does War Create Peace?

Criteria for Robust Integrated Units	Not Yet!	On Our Way!	This Is It!
RELEVANCE • Meaningful • Purposeful • Life experiences • Real	Inert knowledge ***WWII as an event***	Relates conceptually ***War as an historical era***	Real-world application ***Concept of conflict***
RICHNESS • Multilayered • Ambiguous • Multiple intelligences • Depth of content	Contrived to fit ***Pencil-and-paper tasks and tests***	Authentic dimensions ***Simulate the war***	Breadth and depth across intelligences ***Develop a museum***
RELATEDNESS • Genuine overlaps • Intentional • Natural hookups across disciplines	No obvious connections across disciplines ***WWII as isolated event***	Superficial connections across disciplines ***WWII as focus for related projects***	Natural, genuine connections across disciplines ***War as concept in economics, literature, science***
RIGOR • Problem solving • Decision making • Higher-order thinking • Expert performance	Pour and store, recall, and regurgitation ***WWII: Show and Tell***	Challenge: follow rigorous procedures ***WWII: Cause and Effect***	Struggle: getting stuck and getting unstuck ***WWII: Problem solving What ifs . . .***
RECURSIVENESS • Recurs • Applies • Threads through and carries over • Flops back and returns to	Singular opportunity for concept/skill development ***Conflict in context of work***	Multiple opportunities for concept/skill development ***Conflict across contexts***	Transfer of skills and concepts to novel situations through problem solving ***Conflict experienced in the process***

Figure 10.6

SkyLight Professional Development

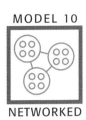

MODEL 10

NETWORKED

Sample of Integrated Unit
Theme/Thread: _Bridging the Way!_

Criteria for Robust Integrated Units	Not Yet!	On Our Way!	This Is It!
RELEVANCE (Real)	Inert knowledge **Bridges (types)**	Relates conceptually to one subject **Bridges in art/architecture & design**	Real-world application **Concept of bridges**
RICHNESS (Multidimensional)	Contrived to fit **Pencil-and-paper tasks and tests about types of bridges**	Singular dimensions **Design, sketch, paint, draw bridges**	Breadth and depth across intelligences **A developed exhibition of models of bridges**
RELATEDNESS (Connected)	No obvious connection across disciplines **Bridges of the world**	Superficial connections across disciplines **Bridges as structures**	Natural, genuine connections across disciplines **Bridges as concept in econ., lit., sci., dev., etc.**
RIGOR (Higher-order thinking)	Pour and store, recall, and regurgitate **Name, locate and describe bridges**	Challenge: follow rigorous procedures **Bridges: making and breaking**	Struggle: getting stuck and getting unstuck **Bridges: Problem-solving What ifs . . .**
RECURSIVENESS (Transfer)	Singular opportunity for concept/skill development **Bridges as architecture**	Multiple opportunities for concept/skill development **Bridges across contexts (conjunctions, transitions)**	Transfer of skills and concepts to novel situations through problem solving **Personally relevant bridges**

Figure 10.7   Extrapolated from Doll, 1993.

BIBLIOGRAPHY

Arredondo, D. E., and R. J. Marzano. 1986. Restructuring schools through the teaching of thinking skills. *Educational Leadership* 43(8):28–30.

Barell, J. 1991. *Teaching for thoughtfulness.* New York: Longman.

Beane, J. 1995. *Toward a coherent curriculum.* Alexandria, VA: Association for Supervision and Curriculum Development.

Bellanca, J. 1990. *The cooperative think tank.* Palatine, IL: Skylight Publishing.

Bellanca, J., and R. Fogarty. 1991. *Blueprints for thinking in the cooperative classroom.* 2d ed. Palatine, IL: SkyLight Publishing.

Beyer, B. 1987. *Practical strategies for the teaching of thinking.* Needham Heights, MA: Allyn & Bacon,

Bloom, A. 1987. *The closing of the American mind.* New York: Simon & Schuster.

Bloom, B. S., ed. 1984. *Taxonomy of educational objectives: The classification of educational goals. Handbook I: Cognitive domain.* New York: Longman.

Brandt, R. 1988. On teaching thinking: A conversation with Arthur Costa. *Educational Leadership* 45(7):10–13.

Brown, R. Q. 1991. *Schools of thought: How the politics of literacy shape thinking in the classroom.* San Francisco: Jossey-Bass.

Bruner, J. 1975. *Toward a theory of instruction.* Cambridge, MA: Belknap Press.

Caine, R. N., and G. Caine. 1990. Understanding a brain-based approach to learning and teaching. *Educational Leadership* 47(2):66–70.

———. 1991. *Making connections: Teaching and the human brain.* Alexandria, VA: Association for Supervision and Curriculum Development.

———. 1994. *Making connections: Teaching and the human brain.* Reading, MA: Addison-Wesley

———. 1997a. *Education on the edge of possibility.* Alexandria, VA: Association for Supervision and Curriculum Development.

———. 1997b. *Unleashing the power of perceptual change: The potential of brain-based teaching.* Alexandria, VA: Association for Supervision and Curriculum Development.

Campbell, L., and B. Campbell. 1999. *Multiple intelligences and student achievement: Success stories from six schools.* Alexandria, VA: Association for Supervision and Curriculum Development.

Carbol, B., project leader. 1990. *The intermediate program: Learning in British Columbia.* Victoria, British Columbia, Canada: Ministry of Education, Educational Programs.

Carr, J. F., and D. Harris. 2001. *Succeeding with standards: Linking curriculum, assessment, and action planning.* Alexandria, VA: Association for Supervision and Curriculum Development.

Costa, A. L. 1991a. Orchestrating the second wave. *Cogitare* 5(2). Palatine, IL: IRI/SkyLight Training and Publishing, Inc.

———. 1991b. *The school as a home for the mind.* Palatine, IL: SkyLight Publishing.

———. 1991c. What human beings do when they behave intelligently and how they can become more so. In *Developing minds: A resource book for teaching thinking.* Vol. I. Alexandria, VA: Association for Supervision and Curriculum Development.

Costa, A. L., and R. Garmstom. 1988. The art of cognitive coaching: Supervision for intelligent teaching. Paper presented at the Annual Conference of the Association for Supervision and Curriculum Development, Chicago.

de Bono, E. 1985. *Six thinking hats.* Boston: Little, Brown and Company.

Drake, S. 1998. *Creating integrated curriculum: Proven ways to increase student learning.* Thousand Oaks, CA: Corwin Press.

Doll, W. 1993. Curriculum possibilities in a "post-future." *Journal of Curriculum and Supervision* 8(4):270–292.

Eisner, E. 1991. What really counts in schools. *Educational Leadership* 48(5):10–11, 14–17.

———. 1994. *Cognition and curriculum reconsidered.* 2d ed. New York: Teachers College Press.

Elvin, L. 1977. *The place of common sense in educational thought.* London: Unwin Educational Books.

Emerson, R. W. 1982. *Selected essays.* New York: Penguin.

Feuerstein, R. 1980. *Instrumental Enrichment.* Baltimore: University Park Press.

Fogarty, R., 1989. From training to transfer: The role of creativity in the adult learner. Ph.D. diss., Loyola University of Chicago.

———. 1990. *Designs for cooperative interactions.* Palatine, IL:, SkyLight Publishing.

———. 1991. Ten ways to integrate curriculum. *Educational Leadership* 49(2): 61–65.

———. 1993. *How to integrate the curricula training manual.* Palatine, IL: IRI/SkyLight Publishing.

———. 2001a. *Differentiated learning: Different strokes for different folks.* Chicago: Fogarty & Associates.

———. 2001b. *Student learning standards: A blessing in disguise.* Chicago: Fogarty & Associates.

———. 2001c. *Teachers make the difference: A framework for quality.* Chicago: Fogarty & Associates.

———. 2002. *Brain-compatible classrooms.* Arlington Heights, IL: SkyLight Professional Development.

Fogarty, R., and J. Bellanca. 1986. *Teach them thinking.* Palatine, IL: SkyLight Publishing.

———. 1989. *Patterns for thinking, patterns for transfer.* Palatine, IL: SkyLight Publishing.

Fogarty, R. and J. Stoehr. 1996. *Integrating curricula with multiple intelligences training manual.* Arlington Heights, IL: IRI/SkyLight Training and Publishing.

Fullan, M. 1991. *The new meaning of educational change.* New York: Teachers College Press.

Gardner, H. 1983. *Frames of mind: The theory of multiple intelligences.* New York: Basic Books.

———. 1999. *Intelligence reframed: Multiple intelligences for the 21st century.* New York: Basic Books.

Glatthorn, A. 1994. *Developing a quality curriculum.* Alexandria, VA: Association for Supervision and Curriculum Development.

Goleman, D. 1995. *Emotional intelligence: Why it can matter more than IQ.* New York: Bantam Books.

Hart, L. 1983. *Human brain, human learning.* Kent, WA: Books for Educators.

Hirsch, E. D., Jr. 1987. *Cultural literacy.* Boston: Houghton-Mifflin.

Hirst, P. H. 1964. *Knowledge and curriculum.* London: Routledge and Kegan Paul.

Hirst, P. H., and R. S. Peters. 1974. The curriculum. In *Conflicting conceptions of curriculum,* edited by E. Eisner and E. Vallance. Berkeley, CA: McCutchen.

Hord, S., and S. Loucks. 1980. *A concerns-based model for delivery of inservice.* Austin: The University of Texas at Austin, CBAM Project, Research and Development Center for Teacher Education.

Howard, D. L. 1994. Interacting with information: Constructing personal knowledge using written text. Ph.D. diss., University of Hawaii at Manoa.

Hunter, M. 1971. *Teach for transfer.* El Segundo, CA: TIP Publications.

Hyde, A., and M. Bizar. 1989. *Thinking in context.* New York: Longman.

Hyerle, D. 1996. *Visual tools for constructing knowledge.* Alexandria, VA: Association for Supervision and Curriculum Development.

Jacobs, H. H., ed. 1989. *Interdisciplinary curriculum: Design and implementation.* Alexandria, VA: Association for Supervision and Curriculum Development.

Jacobs, H. H. 1997. *Mapping the big picture: Integrating curriculum and assessment K–12.* Alexandria, VA: Association for Supervision and Curriculum Development.

Jacobs, H. H., and J. H. Borland. 1986. The interdisciplinary concept model: Theory and practice. *Gifted Child Quarterly* 30(4):159–163.

Jensen, E. 1999. *Teaching with the brain in mind.* Alexandria, VA: Association for Supervision and Curriculum Development.

Jones, B. F., A. Palincsar, D. S. Ogle, and E. G. Carr. 1987. *Strategic teaching and learning: Cognitive instruction in the content areas.* Alexandria, VA: Association for Supervision and Curriculum Development.

Jones, B. F., M. Tinzmann, L. Friedman, and B. Walker. 1987. *Teaching thinking skills: English/language arts.* Washington, DC: National Educational Association.

Joyce, B. R. 1986. *Improving America's schools.* New York: Longman.

Joyce, B. R., and B. Showers. 1980. Improving inservice training: The message of research. *Educational Leadership* 37(5):379–382, 384–385.

———. 1983. *Power and staff development through research and training.* Alexandria, VA: Association for Supervision and Curriculum Development.

Kentucky Educational Television. 1993. *Integrated learning video series* [Videocassettes]. Produced by Kentucky Educational Television.

Kovalic, S. 1993. *ITI: The model: Integrated thematic instruction.* Oak Creek, AZ: Books for Educators.

Lawton, D, 1975. *Class, culture and curriculum.* Boston: Routledge and Kegan Paul.

Lazear, D. 1999. *Eight ways of knowing.* 3d ed. Arlington Heights, IL: SkyLight Training and Publishing.

———. 1999. *Eight ways of teaching.* 3d ed. Arlington Heights, IL: SkyLight Training and Publishing.

Marcus, S. "Are Four Food Groups Enough?" Ph.D. diss., Walden University, n. d.

Martin, H. 1996. *Integrating mathematics across the curriculum.* Arlington Heights, IL: SkyLight Training and Publishing.

Marzano, R. J., D. Pickering, and R. Brandt. 1990. Integrating instruction programs through dimensions of learning. *Educational Leadership* 47(5):17–24.

Maute, J., 1989. Cross-curricular connections. *Middle School Journal,* 20(4):20–22.

Meeth, L. R. 1978. Interdisciplinary studies: Integration of knowledge and experience. *Change* 10: 6–9.

Ministry of Education. 1991. *Integration: A framework for discussion.* Draft #2. Victoria, British Columbia, Canada.

Missouri Department of Elementary and Secondary Education. 1996. *Standards of learning.* Jefferson City, MO.

Osborn, A. F. 1963. *Applied imagination.* New York: Scribner.

Parnes, S. J. 1975. *Aha! Insights into creative behavior.* Buffalo, NY: D.O.K. Publishing.

Perkins, D. N. 1986. *Knowledge as design.* Hillsdale, NJ: Lawrence Erlbaum Associates.

———. 1988. Thinking frames. Paper presented at Association for Supervision and Curriculum Development Conference, Approaches to Teaching Thinking, Alexandria, VA.

———. 1989. Selecting fertile themes for integrated learning. In *Interdisciplinary curriculum: Design and implementation,* edited by H. H. Jacobs. Alexandria, VA: Association for Supervision and Development.

Perkins, D. N., H. Goodrich, S. Tishman, and J. Mirman Owen. 1994. *Thinking connections: Learning to think and thinking to learn.* Reading, MA: Addison-Wesley.

Perkins, D. N., and G. Salomon. 1988. Teaching for transfer. *Educational Leadership* 46(1):22–32.

———. 1989. Are cognitive skills content bound? *Educational Researcher* 18(1):16–25.

Perna, D. M, and J. R. Davis. 2000. *Aligning standards and curriculum for classroom success.* Arlington Heights, IL: SkyLight Training and Publishing.

Pete, B. Forthcoming. *Active brains, engaged minds: Experience the difference.* Chicago: Fogarty & Associates.

Piaget, J. 1972. *The epistemology of interdisciplinary relationships.* Paris: Organization for Economic Cooperation and Development.

Posner, M. I., and S. W. Keele. 1973. Skill learning. In R. M. W. Travers (Ed.). *Second handbook of research on teaching.* Chicago: Rand McNally.

Ravitch, D. 1985. Why educators resist a basic required curriculum. In B. Gross and R. Gross (Eds.). *The great school debate.* New York: Simon and Schuster.

Ravitch, D., and C. Finn. 1985. The humanities: A truly challenging course of study. In B. Gross and R. Gross (Eds.). *The great school debate.* New York: Simon and Schuster.

Resnick, L. B., and L. Klopfer. 1989. *Toward the thinking curriculum: Current cognitive research. 1989 ASCD Yearbook.* Alexandria, VA: Association for Supervision and Curriculum Development.

Richards, M. C., 1980. *The public school and the education of the whole person.* Philadelphia and New York: The Pilgrim Press.

Ronis, D. 2001. *Problem-based learning for math and science: Integrating inquiry and the Internet.* Arlington Heights, IL: SkyLight Training and Publishing.

Sergiovanni, T. 1987. Will we ever have a true profession? *Educational Leadership* 44(8):44–49.

Shoemaker, B. 1989. Integrative education: A curriculum for the twenty-first century. *OSSC Bulletin* 33(2).

———. 1991. Education 2000: Integrated curriculum. *Phi Delta Kappan* 72(10):793–797.

Silver, H., R. Strong, and M. Perini. 2000. *So each may learn: Integrating learning styles and multiple intelligences.* Alexandria, VA: Association for Supervision and Curriculum Development.

Sousa, D. 1995. *How the brain learns: A classroom teacher's guide.* Reston, VA: The National Association of Secondary Schools.

Sprenger, M. 1999. *Learning and memory: The brain in action.* Alexandria, VA: Association for Supervision and Curriculum Development.

Sternberg, R. J. 1984. How can we teach intelligence? *Educational Leadership* 42(1):38–48.

———. 1986. *Intelligence applied: Understanding and increasing your intellectual skills.* New York: Harcourt Brace Jovanovich.

Sylwester, R. 1995. *Celebration of neurons: An educator's guide to the human brain.* Alexandria, VA: Association for Supervision and Curriculum Development.

Treadwell, M. 2001. 1001 *Best Internet sites for educators.* Arlington Heights, IL: SkyLight Professional Development.

Tyler, R. W. 1949. *Basic principles of curriculum and instruction.* Chicago: University of Chicago Press.

———. 1986–1987. The five most significant curriculum events in the twentieth century. *Educational Leadership* 44(4):36–38.

Vars, G. F. 1987. *Interdisciplinary teaching in the middle grades.* Columbus, OH: National Middle School Association.

Wiggins, G., and J. McTighe. 1998. *Understanding by design.* Alexandria, VA: Association for Supervision and Curriculum Development.

Wittrock, M. C. 1967. Replacement and nonreplacement strategies in children's problem solving. *Journal of Educational Psychology* 58(2):69–74.

Index

SkyLight Professional Development

SkyLight

PROFESSIONAL DEVELOPMENT

We Prepare Your Teachers Today for the Classrooms of Tomorrow

Learn from Our Books and from Our Authors!

Ignite Learning in Your School or District.

SkyLight's team of classroom-experienced consultants can help you foster systemic change for increased student achievement.

Professional development is a process not an event. SkyLight's experienced practitioners drive the creation of our on-site professional development programs, graduate courses, research-based publications, interactive video courses, teacher-friendly training materials, and online resources—call SkyLight Professional Development today.

SkyLight specializes in three professional development areas.

Specialty #  **1**
Best Practices

We **model** the best practices that result in improved student performance and guided applications.

Specialty #  **2**
Making the Innovations Last

We help set up **support** systems that make innovations part of everyday practice in the long-term systemic improvement of your school or district.

Specialty #  **3**
How to Assess the Results

We prepare your school leaders to encourage and **assess** teacher growth, **measure** student achievement, and **evaluate** program success.

Contact the SkyLight team and begin a process toward long-term results.

SkyLight
Professional
Development

2626 S. Clearbrook Dr., Arlington Heights, IL 60005
800-348-4474 • 847-290-6600 • FAX 847-290-6609
info@skylightedu.com • www.skylightedu.com